国学经典·处世三奇书

汉英对照
CHINESE-ENGLISH

FIRESIDE TALK AT NIGHT

围炉夜话

[清] 王永彬 / 著
周文标 / 英译
周文标 应佳鑫 / 译注

百花洲文艺出版社
BAIHUAZHOU LITERATURE AND ART PRESS

图书在版编目（CIP）数据

围炉夜话：汉英对照 /（清）王永彬著；周文标英译；周文标，应佳鑫译注.
-- 南昌：百花洲文艺出版社，2020.9
ISBN 978-7-5500-3781-6

Ⅰ.①围… Ⅱ.①王… ②周… ③应… Ⅲ.①个人 – 修养 – 中国 – 清代②《围炉夜话》– 译文 – 汉、英③《围炉夜话》– 注释 – 汉、英 Ⅳ.①B825

中国版本图书馆CIP数据核字（2020）第132003号

围炉夜话：汉英对照

WEI LU YEHUA：HAN-YING DUIZHAO

[清] 王永彬 著　周文标 英译　周文标　应佳鑫 译注

出 版 人	章华荣
责任编辑	郝玮刚　蔡央扬　程慧敏
书籍设计	方　方
制　　作	周璐敏
出版发行	百花洲文艺出版社
社　　址	南昌市红谷滩新区世贸路898号博能中心A座20楼
邮　　编	330038
经　　销	全国新华书店
印　　刷	江西华奥印务有限责任公司
开　　本	787mm × 1092mm 1/16　印张 13.75
版　　次	2020年9月第1版第1次印刷
字　　数	219千字
书　　号	ISBN 978-7-5500-3781-6
定　　价	55.00元

赣版权登字 05-2020-107

走向世界的明清小品
——汉英对照本"处世三奇书"序

The Sketches of the Ming and Qing Dynasties Going Abroad
— Preface to the "Three Canons of Personal Cultivation"

赵丽宏
Zhao Lihong

"处世三奇书"是中国古典文学的汉英对照本。在中国传统文化的出版物中，这是一套体例新颖的双语读本。这个读本，不仅向读者展现了中国古典文学一方迷人的天地，也为对中国文化有兴趣的英语读者提供了一个学习的园圃。读者可以由中文而英文，也可以由英文而中文。研习英文的中国读者，学习中文的外国读者，都可以在其中获得阅读的乐趣。

"Three Canons of Personal Cultivation" is a Chinese-English version of Chinese classical literature. In the publications of Chinese traditional culture, this is a set of bilingual readings with new style. It not only shows the charming world of Chinese classics, but also provides a learning garden for English readers who are interested in Chinese culture. Readers can read the canons in two ways, either from Chinese to English or from English to Chinese. Both Chinese readers who are learning English and foreign readers who are learning Chinese are enabled to get the pleasure of reading them.

《菜根谭》《小窗幽记》和《围炉夜话》是明清时期流传下来的三本以修身养性、劝善励志为中心话题的清言体小品集，作者分别是洪应明、陈继儒和王永彬。因其在同类书中出众的地位和影响力，被世人誉为"处世三奇书"，颇受文人墨客和普通百姓的喜爱。

The Roots of Wisdom, *Meditative Notes in Solitude* and *Fireside Talk at Night* are the three famous books successively appearing in the Ming Dynasty (1368-1644) and the Qing Dynasty (1644-1911), with subjects mainly on moral cultivation and inspirational exhortations on doing good and working hard, and therefore known as the "Three Canons of Personal Cultivation" out of their unparalleled status in books of the same kind and influence among the intellectuals and ordinary people.

　　华夏文化的发展，每个历史时期都有创造性的文学形态，并在各自领域中登峰造极，成为一个时代的文化标记。明清两朝也不例外，在前后五个多世纪里，小说显然是明清时期的一个主要文化特色，其次就是那些饱蕴着智慧才情、展示着世态风情的辑录和承载着先人学说和思想的格言体小品集了。通过这些作品，我们可以清楚地了解到：优秀的文学家，是中国传统文化的脊梁，他们那些形诸文字的精神与情感结晶是中华文明最有生命力的一部分。世风日下依然能倡导并坚持孝悌，物欲横流依然能淡泊名利，仕途得意依然能心存忧患意识，遭遇不测依然能泰然处之，国家危亡依然能竭尽忠诚，温饱之余依然能不忘劳作之苦，生活清贫依然能寄情山水，凡此种种，都是这些优秀文人留给后世的宝贵精神财富。

In the long history of China, cultural development of each era has its own creative literary form and insurmountable height, thus becoming a cultural mark of the time, the same those of the dynasties of Ming and Qing. During more than five centuries, the novels and fictions are of course the primary literary identity of the dynasties, and the collections brimming with human wits and revealing the ways of the world and the compilations of previous classical works, ancestors' quotes and their developed writings must be the next. Through these works and writings, we see clearly that the excellent literati are really the backbone of Chinese classical culture, and that the crystallization of spirit and emotion they created in words is one of the most vivid parts of Chinese civilization. As the breeders of the civilization of that times, even when the general moves were getting worse and worse they would remain faithful to filial piety and fraternal duty;

even when in an acquisitive time they would remain indifferent to fame and wealth; even when content with their official careers they would remain preoccupied with the misery consciousness; even when coming across unexpected occurrences they would remain unruffled and take them calmly; even when the state was in peril they would remain loyal; even when having enough food and clothing they would remain concerned about the pain of labor; even when living a poor life they would remain disposed to bask in the poetic mood between mountains and rivers. — All these refined qualities are the precious spiritual wealth the excellent literati handed down to us later generations.

"处世三奇书"所收纳的短句小品均为清言体，风格相似，读起来朗朗上口，既有诗歌的韵律又有散文的流畅。这些编辑成集、主题鲜明的短句小品，是被柔美化了的格言，似诗非诗，似文非文，是小品文的一种，形式上是介于箴言警句和散文之间的文体，通常由前后对仗或排比的两句或两段组成，以达到均衡与和谐之美。由清言汇集而成的书籍叫清言集或清言体小品集，有分编和不分编两种，题材自由，体例松散，所收清言小品数量少则近百则、多则数百则不等，每则小品的篇幅少则七八个字，多则逾百。内容涵盖古贤经典和民俗文化，其中尤以演绎儒道释三家之言为多，形式短小精致，文风飘逸清雅，具有"小品中的小品（林语堂语）"的美称。

The short sketches contained in the "Three Canons of Personal Cultivation" are all with distinctive themes, clear-spoken, similar in style, easy to read, and full of the rhythm of poetry and fluency of prose. So far as the form is concerned, these sketches belong to a kind of maxims literarily beautified with a manner of seemingly like but actually not a poem or seemingly like but actually not a prose, normally composed of two sentences or two paragraphs adorned with antitheses, couplets and other rhetoric devices to achieve the beauty of balance and harmony, and with its writing style lying between maxim and prose. The collections with such writings are called clear-and-upright sketches, usually there being two ways of compilation, classified or non-classified, either freely with subject matter or loose in layout, in which the pieces collected vary from nearly one hundred to several hundreds, and Chinese characters used in different pieces vary from seven or eight to more than a hundred, and the contents arranged cover Chinese classics and folk culture, mostly related to the sayings derived from the theories of Confucianism, Taoism and Buddhism. They are short in length, vivid in format and elegant in expression, and therefore praised by Mr. Lin Yutang (a famous modern Chinese scholar) as "a mini-sketch of sketches".

  "处世三奇书"的可贵之处在于：三位作者皆以其丰富的学养、渊博的知识、明敏的思辨、冷隽的文字、促人深省的儆诫、益人心智的启迪，以及豁达如禅的觉醒，从古贤经典和民俗文化中撷取菁华但又不简单地复述这些原文，而是在赋予它们一定的情景衬托后将其锻造成一个个既养眼又养心的段子，于寥寥隽语中将经典所含的意旨优雅地展现在读者面前，充分诠释了中国传统文人的文化底蕴和人文情怀，为世人展现了一幅古人修身养性的清晰图景，让读者在诵读这些金科玉律时多了一份愉悦感和亲近感。

The praiseworthiness of the "Three Canons of Personal Cultivation" is as obvious as this: instead of simply quoting the original sayings, the three authors, by applying their rich learning and cultivation, profound knowledge, dialectical thinking, grave and stern expressions, thought-provoking warning, meditative enlightenment and self-awareness, turned out their sketches in the least paradoxes to exemplify the extracts from the classical works and folk culture, and gave prominence to the pieces well matched with relevant scene, sight, circumstances, background or landscape, thus achieving the effect of being pleasant to readers' eyes and minds. Their endeavors fully annotate the cultural deposits and humanistic sensibilities of the traditional literati, and thus enable us to have the opportunity to see a clear picture of the personal cultivation of the ancients, and make us feel more pleasure and intimacy than ever in reading the famous aphorisms of ancient classics.

十年前，周文标先生在上海人民出版社出版发行《菜根谭》汉英对照本时，我曾为他写过一篇序。据我所知，十余年来，他一直不懈地致力于用英文翻译和编撰中国传统典籍，并在呈现方式上做了积极的探索。这次他与百花洲文艺出版社共同成套推出"处世三奇书"汉英对照本，足见他这些年在这方面所倾注的时间和精力。周文标先生是上海市作家协会的会员，我为我们作协有这么一位孜孜不倦向世界推广中国传统文化的同仁感到骄傲。衷心祝贺他的"处世三奇书"汉英对照本成功出版，这是明清小品走向世界的一次积极尝试。期待他有更多新著在不久的将来问世。

10 years ago, when Mr. Zhou Wenbiao's *The Roots of Wisdom* in Chinese-English version was about to be published by Shanghai People's Publishing House, I wrote a preface for him. As I know, Mr. Zhou has been unceasingly spending most of his spare time on translating and compiling Chinese classics in English for more than ten years, and has made an active scrutiny into the modes of presentation. This time, he and Baihuazhou Literature and Art Press jointly plan to issue the "Three Canons of Personal Cultivation" in the form of three-in-one packing, which shows how much time and energy he has devoted in this respect. Mr. Zhou is a member of Shanghai Writers Association, and I am proud to have such a colleague who has been working so tirelessly to introduce Chinese traditional culture to the world. Here I'd like to extend my hearty congratulations on his successful publication of the Chinese-English

"Three Canons of Personal Cultivation", thinking that it is a positive attempt for the sketches of the Ming and Qing Dynasties to go abroad. Furthermore, I'll look forward to seeing his more new works to be published in the near future.

是为序。

It's my pleasure to write this preface as above.

2018 年 7 月 31 日于四步斋

Four-Pace Study in Shanghai
July 31st, 2018

序

Introduction to *Fireside Talk at Night*

周文标

Zhou Wenbiao

寒夜围炉，田家妇子之乐也。顾篝灯坐对，或默默然无一言，或嘻嘻然言非所宜言，皆无所谓乐，不将虚此良夜乎？余识字农人也。岁晚务闲，家人聚处，相与烧煨山芋，心有所得，辄述诸口，命儿辈缮写存之，题曰围炉夜话。但其中皆随得随录，语无伦次浅辞芜，多非信心之论，特以课家人消永夜耳，不足为外人道也。倘蒙有道君子惠而正之，则幸甚。

It is quite a pleasure for the members of a peasant household to sit by the fireside on winter night. Face to face, with eyes gazing at the jack-o'-lantern, they now stay in silence by saying nothing at all, now talk about something inappropriate at ordinary time in a way of laughing or joking, only for the purpose of amusing themselves and not spending the good night in dullness. I'm in fact a farmer of literacy. By the end of the year, when nothing is left to be undone, all my family would get together to roast sweet potato for each other; and in case I am seized by sudden inspiration, I would relate it orally and let my sons to record it, and eventually creating a book titled Fireside Talk at Night. Honestly, what contained in this book are some of my random talks and incoherent speeches without any decoration, many of them are the things I myself am not so confident of, merely for the family to while away the hours in the long winter, not worthy of any attention of outsiders. Nevertheless, it would still be my great honor if someday my book can luckily be rectified by a man of virtue and learning.

以上这段文字传闻是清代文人王永彬为其自撰的《围炉夜话》所写的序，寥寥数语勾勒出了作者著书时的生活背景和心境，使读罢该序的人即刻就会有详读其书的欲望。

The above lines are said to be the preface written by Wang Yongbin himself, a literary man of the Qing Dynasty, for his book of *Fireside Talk at Night*. With words as brief as that, it roughs out the author's living condition and status of the mind in the time he wrote this book, giving birth to the ones the desire to read the whole text immediately after they go over the preface.

王永彬（1792 年—1869 年），字宜山，人称宜山先生，王氏后人称其宜山公，一生经历了乾隆、嘉庆、道光、咸丰、同治五个王朝，享年七十有八。他不喜科举，很晚才恩获贡生科名，为修职郎，参与编修同治版本《枝江县志》，担任"分修"，后候选教谕。因深受儒家思想熏陶，在教学中，先令学生修身，次教其治学，不以科举应试为唯一目的，并能身先士卒，修养己身而后教。同时对于乡人见善必赏；见过必反复规劝，一定要使其彻底改正。他涉猎广泛，在著述授业之余，经史、诸子、书法、医学皆习，尤好吟诗。其同郡文友王柏心为其撰写《勅授修职郎宜山王公传》记载："公著述外，尤好吟咏，与高安周柳溪、彝陵（夷陵）罗梦生结诗社，号吟坛三友。"

Wang Yongbin (1792-1869), styled Yishan and so called Mr. Yishan by the locals and esteemed as the Reverend Mr. Yishan by his descendants, went through five reigns of the Qing Dynasty in life, namely Qianlong, Jiaqing, Daoguang, Xianfeng and Tongzhi, and lived to the age of 78. He personally disliked the system of imperial examination and therefore was very late recommended as a tribute student and then nominated as an assistant editor in charge of compiling *Zhijiang County Annals*, and given the teacher's qualification afterwards. Deeply influenced by Confucianism, he adhered to an idea in his teaching that moral cultivation should go ahead of cultural learning, and never thought the imperial examination was the only purpose of study. Meanwhile, he always paid high attention to cultivating himself when performing education and thus set a very good example for his disciples. In his hometown, he often rewarded those who had done good and more often admonished those who had errors and persisted in doing so till they had corrected them. Besides writing and teaching, he also spent much time to read a big variety of books including Confucian classics, historical records, philosophical writings and miscellaneous works, especially fond of poem chanting. Wang Baixin, one of the author's pen friends of the same prefecture, recorded it in his *Life of the Reverend Mr. Yishan, a Conferred Assistant Editor*, saying, "Apart from authoring books, the Reverend Mr. Yishan had a special hobby in poem chanting, and together with Zhou Liuxi of Gao'an and Luo Mengsheng of Yi Ling, formed a poets' club named the 'Three Companions of Poetic Circle'."

王永彬是个崇尚儒学的学者，修为奉行"立德、立功、立言"三不朽理念，所著《围炉夜话》凡184则，为"处世三奇书"的第三部。该书儒家色彩浓重，十分注重和强调儒教所倡导的、更具人生要义的耕读文化，对类似"竹林七贤"的玄学新风以及历朝历代离群索居、遗世独立的隐士做派多有不屑和针砭，个别篇幅甚至还有蔑视和贬低道佛墨杨四家的倾向，学术立场和意见不可谓不分明。但是尽管如此，书中涉及道德、修身、读书、安贫乐道、教子、忠孝、勤俭等多方面的锦言佳句却丝毫未减作者的智慧和人性光芒，对当代读者仍有颇多启迪。

Wang Yongbin advocated Confucianism all his life and pursued the realization of immortality in cultivating virtue, making achievements and establishing arguments. His book of *Fireside Talk at Night* is chronologically listed the third one of the "Three Canons of Personal Cultivation", containing 184 pieces of sketches in all. With heavy Confucianist overtones, the book he wrote especially emphasizes the concept of farming and reading proposed and considered much more important than anything else in life by Confucians. It disdains and criticizes at the same time the metaphysics of the Seven Worthies of the Bamboo Grove and the style and methods of those solitary recluses in the past dynasties, and even shows little inclination to agree with the views of Taoism, Buddhism, Moism and Yang Zhu in certain sketches, whereby we know clearly his academic position and opinion. But even so, the brilliance of his wisdom and humanity in his sayings about morality, personal cultivation, learning, contentment in poverty and devotion to the Tao, family education, loyalty and filiality, hardworking and practicing thriftiness is in no way diminished, and there are still many enlightenments for contemporary readers.

2017 年 9 月于上海

Shanghai, China
September, 2017

1. 教于幼正大光明 检于心忧勤惕厉 /001

1. To educate children, we'd better cultivate their honesty and integrity; to examine ourselves, we'd better do it with diligence and self-encouragement.

2. 学朋友长处 习圣贤言语 /002

2. Learn strong points from our friends and practice the teachings of sages.

3. 俭以济贫 勤能补拙 /003

3. Be frugal to survive your poverty and diligent to make up for your dullness.

4. 稳当话也即平常话 本分人也即快活人 /004

4. Proper words are ordinary words; dutiful persons are happy persons.

5. 处事为人作想 读书须己用功 /005

5. In dealing with affairs, think for others; when engaged in learning, do it with concentration yourself.

6. 信是立身之本 恕乃接物之要 /006

6. Credibility is the essence of life while tolerance is the key to association.

7. 说话而杀身 积财而丧命 /007

7. You will be endangered if you are too talkative or accumulate too much wealth.

8. 严可平躁 敬以化邪 /008

8. Strictness helps to restrain impetuous dispositions; courtesy helps to dissolve evil thoughts.

9. 勤修恒业 审定章程 /009

9. Rules and regulations must be observed in managing a family enterprise.

10. 名利不可贪 学业在德行 /010

10. Undeserved fame and gain must not be coveted; academic achievement lies in morality.

11. 古朴君子力挽江河 名节之士光争日月 /011

11. A man of integrity is he who can stem the current trend; a man of honor is he who can compete with the sun and moon.

12. 心正见神明 人生无安逸 /012

12. A man who keeps his heart properly will have the aid of deities; there are no ease and comfort in real life.

13. 人心足恃 天道好还 /013

13. The will of a true man can always be counted on; heavenly retribution, good or bad, is bound to come in turn.

14. 有才者如浑金璞玉 为学者如行云流水 /016

14. A talented man should be like

unrefined gold and uncut jade and like flowing water and floating cloud, the man of learning.

15. 积善有余庆 积财易遗祸 /017

15. The accumulation of goodness brings about good fortune while the accumulation of wealth invites calamity.

16. 要以德化人 勿以财累己 /018

16. Influence others with virtue and don't let your wealth weigh you down.

17. 读书无论资性高低 立身不嫌家世贫贱 /020

17. Aptitude is not a decisive factor in study; poor family status does not affect personal establishment.

18. 恶乡愿 弃鄙夫 /021

18. Stay away from hypocrites and despise vulgarians.

19. 精明败家风 朴实振家业 /022

19. Too much astuteness in social dealings ruins family reputation; plainness and honesty revitalize family businesses.

20. 明辨是非 不忘廉耻 /023

20. To be a man, one should distinguish right from wrong and keep in his heart the sense of shame.

21. 愚忠愚孝不可取 假仁假义要不得 /024

21. Neither foolish loyalty and filial piety nor sham benevolence and righteousness are advisable.

22. 权势如烟云过眼 奸邪无事生非 /025

22. Power and influence are floating clouds; an evil man makes trouble out of nothing.

23. 不为富贵所动 常将忠孝记挂 /026

23. Never be moved by wealth and rank and always keep in mind loyalty and filiality.

24. 物命可惜 人心可回 /027

24. Lives of the all living beings under heaven are worth cherishing.

25. 处事论是非 立言贵精详 /028

25. In handling affairs, one should be clear about right and wrong, and attentive to intensiveness and thoroughness in writing and speaking.

26. 有科名心 无济世才 /029

26. There are some who only have the heart to gain scholarship but no ability to govern and serve.

27. 静而止闹 淡而消窘 /030

27. Motionlessness can calm down disturbance while plainness can avoid embarrassment.

28. 行善救人 脱身俗情 /031

28. Be willing to help others and one will break away from poor taste.

29. 气性乖张短命 言语尖刻薄福 /032

29. Those who are eccentric and often behave in a queer way are short of longevity and luck.

30. 胸怀大志 脚踏实地 /033

30. We should not only be ambitious, but also down-to-earth.

31. 贫贱不能移 富贵要济世 /034

31. Remain unyielding when poor; be useful to the world when rich.

32. 即物穷理 名副其实 /035

32. To derive the implications from the name of a subject is always advisable.

33. 以身作则 心平气和 /037

33. In daily life, we must make ourselves an example and be gentle with others.

34. 不贻羞于父母 勿贻害于子孙 /038

34. Don't do anything stupid to shame your parents and injure your offspring.

35. 待人不可势利 习业万勿粗心 /039

35. Don't be snobbish in dealing with others; don't be careless in doing things.

36. 不妄自尊大 要奋发图强 /040

36. Strive to be strong, not arrogant.

37. 东山可再起 江心补漏迟 /041

37. Failure can make a comeback.

38. 生命有穷期 学问无止境 /042

38. Life must have its end while knowledge has no limit.

39. 做事要问心无愧 创业需量力而行 /043

39. Things need to be done with a clear conscience; Entrepreneurship needs to be done according to one's ability.

40. 气性乖张无足取 言语矫饰属可疑 /044

40. It is undesirable to be eccentric and questionable.

41. 守拙可取 交友宜慎 /045

41. It's quite advisable to remain free from ambition and careful in making friends.

42. 放眼读书 立跟做人 /046

42. Be open-minded when reading; stand firm to be a man.

43. 持身贵严 处世贵谦 /047

43. Solemnness is valuable in conducting oneself, so is modesty in dealing with the world.

44. 善用其财 无愧其禄 /048

44. It will bring you no shame if you can make a good use of your salary.

45. 交益友 立品行 /049

45. It's better to make helpful friends and behave yourself properly.

46. 君子如神 小人如鬼 /050

46. The man of virtue is like a deity and a ghost, the man of no virtue.

47. 严以律己 宽以待人 /051

47. Be strict with yourself and lenient with others.

48. 守口如瓶 持身若璧 /052

48. Keep your mouth as tight as a bottle and be yourself as pure as jade.

49. 不较横逆 安守贫穷 /053

49. Overlook the importunate persons and be content with poverty.

50. 白云山岳皆文章 黄花松柏乃吾师 /055

50. White clouds and high mountains are all good texts; chrysanthemums and pines are my examples.

51. 行善自乐 奸谋自坏 /056

51. The person who is willing to help others entertains himself; the fellow who hatches a plot can be ruined by his own plot.

52. 以人为镜 防微杜渐 /057

52. To practice precaution, take human as mirror.

53. 谨守规模 必无大错 /058

53. Act according to the public conventions and one will make no big mistake.

54. 耐得住烦 吃得起亏 /059

54. Be patient in everything and ready to suffer losses at any time.

55. 习读书业 知读书乐 /060

55. Taking learning as a lifetime hobby, one should know the pleasure in it.

56. 知己不足 学业日进 /061

56. Only when you are aware of your shortcomings can you study hard and make progress every day.

57. 敬人者人恒敬之 靠人者莫若靠己 /062

57. To respect others is to respect yourself; to rely on others is no better than to rely on yourself.

58. 学长者助人之道 识君子修己之功 /063

58. Learn the way of helping others from the elders and from the men of virtue, the way of moral cultivation.

59. 奢侈悭吝俱可败家 庸愚精明都能覆事 /064

59. Luxury is enough to dissipate a family, so is stinginess; stupidity is enough to spoil a thing, so is astuteness.

60. 安守本业 不合浊流 /065

60. Do your own business and never go with the turbid current.

61. 衣食比下有余 学业比上不足 /066

61. It's not desirable to be worse off than some in study and better off than many in daily life.

62. 富不骄纵 贫不改志 /067

62. Don't be arrogant when you are rich; don't change your mind whether you are poor.

63. 富贵要谦恭 衣禄需俭省 /069

63. Be modest when getting rich and powerful, and frugal when carefree of food and clothing.

64. 作善降祥 不善降殃 /070

64. Good luck will call on you if you show mercy while bad luck will do so if you do evil.

65. 和平处事 正直居心 /071

65. Live peacefully with the world and be fair and upright yourself.

66. 君子拯救尘世 圣贤关心民生 /072

66. It's a duty for a man of virtue to save the world and take care about the people, for a sage.

67. 偷安败家 争赀必伤 /074

67. Indulgence in ease and comfort is to ruin the family; scrambling for family properties is to injure the kindred.

68. 沉实谦恭兴业 忠厚勤俭兴家 /075

68. Being steady and modest makes a business prosperous; being honest and diligent makes a family flourish.

69. 莲朝开而暮合 草冬枯而春荣 /076

69. Lotus flowers bloom in the morning and shut in the evening; grasses flourish in spring and wither in winter.

70. 自伐自矜当戒 我自求仁求义 /077

70. Guard against the habit of boasting and cultivate yourself with benevolence and righteousness.

71. 贫寒更须读书 富贵不忘稼穑 /078

71. Study harder when poor and don't forget the hardship of farmwork when rich.

72. 俭可养廉 静能生悟 /079

72. Thrift helps to nourish the character of incorruptibility; quiet helps to breed the sense of the world.

73. 助人在于有心 虑事在于精详 /080

73. Helping others is all about the heart; considering a thing is all about the accurateness and carefulness.

74. 常怀振奋心 多说切直话 /081

74. Always keep in mind your lofty aspirations and speak as earnestly as you can.

75. 虚怀若谷即才德 骄奢淫逸枉富贵 /082
75. It's a virtue to be modest and a shame to be arrogant when rich and powerful.

76. 凝浩然正气 法古今完人 /084
76. Cultivate yourself with uprightness and learn from the men of perfect morality.

77. 饱暖则气昏志惰 饥寒则神紧骨坚 /085
77. People tend to be indolent when well fed and will be firm-minded when hungry and cold.

78. 愁烦中具潇洒襟怀 暗昧处见光明世界 /086
78. Be easy and unrestrained when in a bad mood and open and above board when in a benighted circumstance.

79. 势利人行为虚假 虚浮者一事无成 /087
79. A snob behaves falsely while a pompous fellow can be nowhere.

80. 不忮不求 勿忘勿助 /088
80. Be neither jealous nor covetous of what others have; keep the heart quiet and let it be as it was.

81. 求其理则数难违 守其常变亦能御 /089
81. Man's fate is predestined and irresistible; stick to the routine, and no unforeseen event cannot be dealt with.

82. 和气为祥 骄气为衰 /090
82. Gentleness stands for the auspiciousness while arrogance, the decline.

83. 人生不可安闲 日用必须简省 /092
83. One should not rest content with a leisurely life but should be frugal in daily life.

84. 卓有成就 铁面无私 /093
84. To make a great achievement, one must be selfless and fearless.

85. 责己不责人则成 信己不信人则败 /094
85. Blaming only oneself rather than others produces success; believing only in oneself rather than others results in failure.

86. 通达事理 无做作气 /095
86. Be a man who is full of sense and unaffected.

87. 正直之心 留名后世 /096
87. Be a man of integrity and make a good name for yourself after death.

88. 后天需努力 小节要谨慎 /097
88. Do work hard and be cautious about the trifles.

89. 忠厚受人尊敬 平淡趣味深长 /098
89. Loyalness is worth respecting while plainness has more taste.

90. 交正直友 学德高人 /099
90. Make friends with honest people and follow the men of high moral character.

91. 解邻里纷争 说因果关系 /100
91. Disputes between neighbors should be settled through explanation of the rotation of karma.

92. 发达需要努力 福寿也靠积德 /101
92. Development and flourishing need efforts; fortune and longevity depend on virtue.

93. 百善孝为先 万恶淫为首 /102
93. Filial piety is the most important of all virtues; Lewdness is the worst of all sins.

94. 自奉减几分 处世退一步 /103
94. In getting along with others,

it's better to conduct yourself in a concessive way.

95. 持守本分安贫乐道 凡事忍让长久不衰 /104

95. Know your poverty and remain happy; forbear for long-term prosperity.

96. 境遇无常 光阴易逝 /105

96. Man's lot is changeable and fleet, man's life.

97. 川学海而至海 莠似苗而非苗 /106

97. All the rivers follow the sea's example and run into it; bristle grasses seem to be but are not seedlings of cereal crops.

98. 守身必谨严 养心须淡泊 /107

98. Man's integrity must be maintained with great care while cultivation of the mind needs no fame and fortune.

99. 有德不在有位 能行不在能言 /108

99. It's important to have noble virtues rather than noble ranks and the ability to act rather than the ability to speak.

100. 称誉易 无怨难 /109

100. It is easy to win praise but hard to avoid resentment.

101. 多记先贤格言 闲看他人行事 /110

101. Keep in heart the teachings of ancient sages and observe the ways of others to act.

102. 身为重臣而精勤 面临大敌犹弈棋 /111

102. An important official in the land should know how to keep calm in the face of a strong enemy.

103. 有济人之心 无欺人之意 /113

103. One should have the heart to donate others rather than the intention to bully them.

104. 能读书即有福 教子弟即创家 /114

104. To read and learn is to invite happiness; to educate kids is to build the family.

105. 教子勿溺爱 子堕莫弃绝 /115

105. Don't spoil your children and give them up when they degenerate.

106. 专心可立功 偏见易败事 /117

106. Concentration is the road to success; prejudice is a slippery slope.

107. 不忘艰难之境 不存侥幸之心 /118

107. Don't forget the existence of adversity and take chances in doing things.

108. 心静则明 品超斯远 /119

108. Man's heart will be clear the minute it calms down; a noble character can rise above the material desires.

109. 贫乃顺境 俭即丰年 /120

109. Poverty is good for reading; frugality is equivalent to abundance.

110. 常有正直心 莫有浮华志 /121

110. Be honest and down-to-earth but don't be hollow and superficial.

111. 异端背乎经常 邪说涉于虚诞 /122

111. Things against the set norms and conventions are called heterodoxy and those relating to fabrication and preposterousness are called heresy.

112. 亡羊尚可补牢 羡鱼何如结网 /124

112. It's never too late to mend the fold even after the sheep is lost; to stand by a river to dream of fish is not as good as going home to knit fishnet.

113. 道本足于身 境难足于心 /125

113. Substance in human nature

is resourceful for moral cultivation; material affluence can hardly satisfy man's heart.

114. 下苦功读书 有益于社会 /126

114. To benefit the world, one must study hard.

115. 知错即改 不甘堕落 /127

115. Correct the mistake when you know it and never abandon yourself to vice.

116. 淡中交耐久 静里寿延长 /128

116. Plain fellowship will ever last; life in peace will be prolonged.

117. 深思熟虑 以绝后患 /129

117. To prevent future trouble, one must think carefully before acting.

118. 聪明不外露 耕读可兼营 /130

118. Farm work and academic study can run side by side.

119. 享受适可而止 学问永不知足 /131

119. One should know how far to go in seeking enjoyment and never be satisfied in learning.

120. 勿与人争 惟求己知 /132

120. Avoid competing with others about gains and losses only to increase your knowledge and ability.

121. 既中规中矩 又灵活变化 /133

121. In social dealings, one should be both disciplined and flexible.

122. 山水是文章化境 烟云乃富贵幻形 /134

122. The mountains and waters are the magic subjects in literature.

123. 察人伦留心细微 化乡风道义为本 /135

123. To observe the world interpersonally is to find out its small problems; to cultivate the countryside is to promote its moral education.

124. 勿妄行欺诈 不独享安闲 /136

124. Don't cheat others and enjoy leisure alone.

125. 忍让非懦弱 自大终糊涂 /137

125. He who practices forbearance is never a coward; he who thinks himself important is after all a blunderer.

126. 功德文章 传诸后世 /138

126. What can be passed on to later generations is only a man's deeds and words.

127. 闭目养心 口阖防祸 /139

127. Close your eyes to nourish the heart; close your mouth to prevent disasters.

128. 富贵难教子 贫穷要读书 /140

128. It's difficult for rich people to bring up their children properly; poor scholars should be devoted to their academic pursuit.

129. 苟且不能振 庸俗不可医 /141

129. People who don't do their business can't cheer up; people of low taste can never be redeemed.

130. 有雄才者 必有大志 /142

130. A man of great talent must have great ambition

131. 让退一步 容易处事 /143

131. When a thing becomes difficult to deal with, a step back can make it easy.

132. 无学为贫 无德为孤 /144

132. Poverty is the lack of knowledge; loneliness is that of virtue.

133. 知过能改 抑恶扬善 /145

133. Correct the mistake when you know it and you can shun evil and

promote good.

134. 诗书立业 孝悌做人 /146

134. Classics are the basis of a man of knowledge and filial piety the pedestal of a man of virtue.

135. 得意勿忘形 苦心终有报 /147

135. Don't get dizzy with success; you will be rewarded if you have done your best and most.

136. 自知之明 不卑不亢 /148

136. People should know themselves well and be neither haughty nor humble.

137. 有为之士不轻为 好事之人非晓事 /149

137. A promising person is one who never act recklessly while a troublemaker one who has no common sense.

138. 勿因噎废食 莫讳疾忌医 /150

138. We should not give up eating for fear of choking and refuse to accept treatment for fear that others will know about our illness.

139. 幕中之宾 座上之客 /151

139. A trusted person is admitted to participating in decision-making; a distinguished guest is worth inviting to take a prominent seat.

140. 种田须尽力 读书要专心 /152

140. Do your best in the field and concentrate your efforts on study.

141. 要栽培子弟 勿暴殄天物 /153

141. Bring up your children with care and don't let things go to waste.

142. 和气待人 藏器待时 /154

142. Treat others kindly and don't use your talent till the right time comes.

143. 大好光阴 切莫错过 /155

143. Don't miss the good time when it is with you.

144. 不失良心 但行正路 /156

144. Keep conscience only to follow the right path.

145. 务本业者常乐 当大任者常忧 /157

145. He who focuses on his own business is always happy; he who is in charge always worried.

146. 求死难救 求福在己 /158

146. It's hard to save a person who is determined to end his life; to seek happiness, do it by oneself.

147. 身不正难有好子弟 依势者必有真对头 /159

147. Your children will behave well if you yourself stand straight; bully others on another's strength and one will bring in enemies for himself.

148. 为学要静敬 教人去骄惰 /160

148. To learn is to make yourself quiet and respectful; to educate people is to get rid of their complacency and laziness.

149. 面对知己无愧 读书要能致用 /161

149. Be worthy of your confidant and practice what you have learned.

150. 直道教人 诚心待人 /162

150. Educate people to follow the right path and treat them with sincerity.

151. 粗粝能甘 纷华不染 /163

151. Be a man who can live a simple life and resist the temptation of wealth and rank.

152. 性情执拗 不可谋事 /164

152. One cannot collaborate with those who are of stubborn temperament.

and kill as well.

173. 身体力行 集思广益 /186

173. To solve a problem collectively, one should do it without letup and listen to all the useful opinions.

174. 种田读书 皆成其业 /187

174. Farm work and study for officialdom are the two ways to earn a living.

175. 儒者多文为富 君子疾名不称 /188

175. A Confucian scholar takes the productiveness of his writings as wealth; an accomplished man is always afraid that he cannot live up to his reputation.

176. 博学笃志 神闲气静 /189

176. Learn widely and aspire steadfastly; be calm-minded and mild-mannered.

177. 规我过者益友 偏私我者小人 /190

177. He who admonishes me of my errors is a helpful friend and a mean fellow, he who only pursues his own ends.

178. 待人宜宽 行礼宜厚 /191

178. Be lenient when treating with others and generous when sending gifts.

179. 观已然而知未然 /192

179. Look at what has happened, and you will know what will happen.

180. 观规模之大小 知事业之高卑 /193

180. Look at its size effect, and you will know if an enterprise is flourishing or declining.

181. 君子尚义 小人趋利 /194

181. A gentleman upholds morality and justice while a mean fellow pursues interests.

182. 小心谨慎无咎 高位难保其终 /195

182. Be careful to avoid error, for superiority gained through a high position cannot last long.

183. 勿以耕读谋富贵 /196

183. One should not take farm work and academic research as the means to accumulate riches and glory.

184. 富而不懂布置则耻 /197

184. It's a shame if one wishes to make plenty of money but know not how to use it.

1. 教于幼正大光明　检于心忧勤惕厉

1. To educate children, we'd better cultivate their honesty and integrity; to examine ourselves, we'd better do it with diligence and self-encouragement.

教子弟^①于幼时，便当有正大光明气象^②；检^③身心^④于平日，不可无忧勤惕厉^⑤工夫。

【中文注释】　　① 子弟：泛指子女、孩子或者学生。
　　　　　　　② 气象：此处指人的言行举止。
　　　　　　　③ 检：检讨；反省。
　　　　　　　④ 身心：指一个人的所言所行和所思所想。
　　　　　　　⑤ 忧勤惕厉：担忧不够勤奋，戒惧无所砥砺。

【今文解译】　　教育孩子要从他们年幼时开始抓起，这样才能培养出他们正直磊落的品质。
　　　　　　　检点自己的思想和行为要从日常抓起，万万不可有任何的松懈和麻痹大意。

【English Translation】

To educate children, we should start it when they are young, so as not to miss the right time to cultivate their honesty and integrity.
In everyday life, we should consciously examine our own deeds and thoughts with diligence and self-encouragement.

2. 学朋友长处　习圣贤言语

2. Learn strong points from our friends and practice the teachings of sages.

　　与朋友交游，须将他好处留心学来，方能受益；对圣贤言语，必要在平时照样行去，才算读书。

【今文解译】　　与朋友交往，一定要留心学习他们的长处，这样才能从中受益。

对圣贤之言，必须要在平日里照样践行，这样才是真正的读书。

【English Translation】

When getting along with our friends, we must give heed to learning strong points from them, so that we can improve ourselves thereby.

When having learned the teachings of a sage, we must put them into practice completely; only in this way can our learning be counted on.

3. 俭以济贫 勤能补拙

3. Be frugal to survive your poverty and diligent to make up for your dullness.

贫无可奈惟求俭，拙亦何妨只要勤。

【今文解译】 穷得走投无路时，唯有节衣缩食才能渡过难关。
头脑愚笨没关系，只要勤奋学习就可弥补不足。

【English Translation】

When bogged down in stricken poverty, the best way to have it out is to practice thrift.

Don't mind the slow-wittedness of your own; try harder and you will be well approved.

4. 稳当话也即平常话　本分人也即快活人

4. Proper words are ordinary words; dutiful persons are happy persons.

稳当^①话，却是平常话，所以听稳当话者不多；本分^②人，即是快活人，无奈做本分人者甚少。

【中文注释】　　① 稳当：稳妥贴切。
　　　　　　　　② 本分：安分守己。

【今文解译】　　妥帖的话也即平常的话，所以听得进妥帖话的人不多。
　　　　　　　　本分的人也即快乐的人，只可惜愿做本分人的人太少。

【English Translation】

Proper words are what called ordinary words; that's why those who are unwilling to pay heed to them are many.

Dutiful persons are what called happy persons; but it's a regret that those who are ready to stick to their duties are few.

5. 处事为人作想　读书须己用功

5. In dealing with affairs, think for others; when engaged in learning, do it with concentration yourself.

处事要代人作想，读书须切己用功。

【今文解译】　为人处事要设身处地为他人着想。
读书学习要自己扎扎实实下功夫。

【English Translation】

In dealing with affairs, one should considerate others' interests.
When engaged in learning, one should concentrate his efforts on it.

6. 信是立身之本 恕乃接物之要

6. Credibility is the essence of life while tolerance is the key to association.

一信字是立身之本，所以人不可无也；一恕字是接物之要，所以终身可行也。

【今文解译】 诚信是做人的根本，所以人不可不讲诚信。
　　　　　　　宽容是处世的要诀，所以人需一辈子践行。

【English Translation】

Credibility is the essence of life, because no one can live or work without it. Tolerance is the key to association; everyone should have it as a lifetime practice.

7. 说话而杀身　积财而丧命

7. You will be endangered if you are too talkative or accumulate too much wealth.

　　人皆欲会说话，苏秦①乃因会说而杀身；人皆欲多积财，石崇②乃因多积财而丧命。

【中文注释】　　① 苏秦，战国时著名的纵横家、外交家和谋略家。口才极佳，游说六国合纵以抗秦，曾一度受封为六国宰相，使秦国不敢窥函谷关有十五年之久，后至齐，从事反间活动，被齐国众大夫因争宠派人刺杀。
② 石崇，西晋时期文学家、大臣、富豪，"金谷二十四友"之一。永康元年（300 年），贾后等为赵王司马伦所杀，司马伦党羽孙秀向石崇索要其宠妾绿珠不果，因而诬陷其为乱党，遭夷三族。晋惠帝复位后，以九卿礼安葬石崇。

【今文解译】　　谁都想能说会道，可是战国的苏秦却因为太会说话而惨遭刺杀。
谁都想发家致富，可是西晋的石崇却因为敛财太多而命丧黄泉。

【English Translation】

Everyone wishes to have a glib tongue, disregarding the fact that Su Qin* was assassinated for his gift of the gab.
Everyone desires to be a richer, not knowing that Shi Chong* was killed for his over-accumulated wealth.

【English Annotation】

* Su Qin (?-317BC), a statesman, diplomat, political strategist during the Warring States Period, and one of the leading figures of the School of Diplomacy (or School of Vertical and Horizontal Alliances), also called Su Zi.
* Shi Chong (249-300), a man of letters as well as a powerful and rich man of the Western Jin Dynasty.

8. 严可平躁　敬以化邪

8. Strictness helps to restrain impetuous dispositions; courtesy helps to dissolve evil thoughts.

教小儿宜严，严气足以平躁气；待小人宜敬，敬心可以化邪心。

【今文解译】　管教孩子一定要严格，严格了才能够去除他们的浮躁气性。
　　　　　　　对待小人一定要客气，客气了就可以化解他们的邪恶心思。

【English Translation】

It's better to educate children with strictness, for strictness can help them restrain their impetuous dispositions.
It's better to treat petty men with courtesy, for courtesy can dissolve their evil thoughts.

9. 勤修恒业　审定章程

9. Rules and regulations must be observed in managing a family enterprise.

　　善谋生者，但令长幼内外，勤修恒业，而不必富其家；善处事者，但就是非可否，审定章程，而不必利于己。

【今文解译】　善于管理家业的人，不必非得为家里增添财富不可，但必须要使家中的男女老少，不论是在家的还是在外的，都能勤勤恳恳地为家业做好各自的事情。
善于处理事情的人，不必因为事情对自己有利才去做，但必须要就事情的对与错该如何鉴别和审定预先订立公正可行的章程，以便有关人等共同遵守。

【English Translation】

A man who is good at managing his family enterprise does not have to bend too much to the affluence of it, but has to instruct all the family members, old and young, inside and outside, to apply themselves hard to their duties in daily activities.

A man who is well versed in handling affairs does not have to do things only in the interest of his own, but has to establish and inspect in his community or circles the rules and regulations of right and wrong for the sake of justice.

10. 名利不可贪　学业在德行

10. Undeserved fame and gain must not be coveted; academic achievement lies in morality.

　　名利之不宜得者竟得之，福终为祸；困穷之最难耐者能耐之，苦定回甘。生资①之高在忠信，非关机巧②；学业之美在德行，不仅文章。

【中文注释】　　① 生资: 人的资质; 人的品质。
　　　　　　　　② 机巧: 算计; 小聪明。

【今文解译】　　不该得到的名利竟然得到了, 这种福分终究会变成祸患;
　　　　　　　　最难熬的贫困熬过去了, 最后肯定会苦尽甘来。
　　　　　　　　人品高贵不在于弄巧玩术, 而在于忠诚信实; 学业精深不
　　　　　　　　仅仅表现在文章上, 而且还反映在德行修为上。

【 English Translation 】

Undeserved fame and gain will finally change into a mishap even though you are already in the possession of them. If you can bravely endure destitution, all the bitterness you go through shall be replaced by sweetness.
Whether the aptitude of a man is high or not is not decided by adroitness but by faithfulness and honesty. The beauty of a man's academic achievement lies not only in writings but also in morality.

11. 古朴君子力挽江河　名节之士光争日月

11. A man of integrity is he who can stem the current trend; a man of honor is he who can compete with the sun and moon.

　　风俗日趋于奢淫，靡所底止^①，安得有敦古朴之君子，力挽江河^②；人心日丧其廉耻，渐至消亡，安得有讲名节之大人，光争日月。

【中文注释】　　① 靡所底止：目前尚无结束的迹象。
　　　　　　　　② 力挽江河：也即力挽狂澜。

【今文解译】　　世风正在变得越来越奢靡，且丝毫没有到头的迹象。怎么才能找到一位崇尚古代敦厚质朴美德的正人君子，来改变当下的局面并开创美好的未来？
　　　　　　　　世人正一天天丧失廉耻之心，都渐渐地变得不知廉耻起来；哪里才能找到一位重视名节的高德之士，来为芸芸众生树立一个堪与日月争辉的榜样？

【English Translation】

The public morals are getting more and more extravagant and self-indulgent, and so far, there have been no indications that the situation will come to a stop. Under such circumstances, couldn't it be a good luck for us to have a man with traditional integrity who is able to stem the current trend and start a new departure?

The masses are morally sinking lower day by day, and if so going on continuously they may lose the sense of dignity and shame in the end. With this in mind, how can we not expect a great man of honor and glory to come out boldly to awake the multitude and be their model as shining as the sun and moon?

12. 心正见神明　人生无安逸

12. A man who keeps his heart properly will have the aid of deities; there are no ease and comfort in real life.

人心统耳目官骸①，而于百体为君②，必随处见神明之宰；人面合眉眼鼻口，以成一字曰苦（两眉为草，眼横鼻直而下承口，乃苦字也），知终身无安逸之时③。

【中文注释】　　① 官骸：意指人的身体器官。
　　　　　　　　② 百体为君：（心是）人体所有器官之首。
　　　　　　　　③ 后半句由于无法用英语作类比，故转译成："人的脸上有眉眼鼻口，如果终日愁苦而不能自遣，人生就永无安逸。"

【今文解译】　　人的心统辖耳朵眼睛等各个器官，是人体的主宰；因此，时刻保持正常的心态，就随处都能得到神明的眷顾。
　　　　　　　　人的脸上有眉毛、眼睛、鼻子和嘴巴，组合在一起像个"苦"字（两道眉毛比作草字头，横着的眼睛和竖着的鼻子正对着下面的口，这不就是个"苦"字吗?！）；由此可知，人的一生是没有安逸可言的。

【English Translation】

Man's heart is the master of human body, governing ears, eyes and all other physical organs. So long as a man can keep his heart properly, wherever he goes, he will have the aid of deities.

Man's face is composed of eyebrows, eyes, nose and mouth; if they are consumed with bitterness all day long, then no ease and comfort can ever be expected for life.

13. 人心足恃　天道好还

13. The will of a true man can always be counted on; heavenly retribution, good or bad, is bound to come in turn.

　　伍子胥^①报父兄之仇，而郢都灭；申包胥^②救君上之难，而楚国存。可知人心足恃也。

　　秦始皇^③灭东周之岁^④，而刘邦^⑤生；梁武帝^⑥灭南齐之年，而侯景^⑦降。可知天道好还也。

【中文注释】　　① 伍子胥（公元前 559 年—公元前 484 年），春秋末期吴国大夫、军事家。伍子胥之父伍奢为楚平王子建太傅，因受费无极谗害，和其长子伍尚一同被楚平王杀害，伍子胥从楚国逃到吴国。公元前 506 年，伍子胥协同孙武带兵攻入楚都，伍子胥掘楚平王墓，鞭尸三百，以报父兄之仇。

② 申包胥（?—?），春秋时期楚国大夫。公元前 506 年，伍子胥率吴军攻打楚国时前往秦国请兵，吴国因受秦楚夹击而退兵。复国后，楚昭王要封赏申包胥，他坚持不受，带一家老小退居山林。

③ 秦始皇（公元前 259 年—公元前 210 年），姓嬴名政，十三岁继承王位，三十九岁称帝，在位三十七年。中国历史上著名的政治家、战略家、改革家，首位完成华夏大一统的铁腕政治人物。

④ 灭东周之岁：据史料记载，东周纪年始于公元前 770 年，到了秦庄襄王元年（即公元前 249 年），东周君欲趁秦连丧昭襄、孝文二王合纵伐秦，秦庄襄王以吕不韦为大将，起兵十万，执东周君而归，尽收巩城等七邑。周朝至此彻底灭亡。据此，"灭东周之岁"应该是公元前 249 年（也即刘邦出生后的第 7 年）；灭东周的不是秦始皇（公元前 246 年才继位），而是当时刚登基的秦庄襄王。——作者引用有误，特予更正。

⑤ 刘邦（公元前 256 年—公元前 195 年），汉朝开国皇

帝, 汉民族和汉文化伟大的开拓者之一、中国历史上杰出
的政治家、卓越的战略家。

⑥ 梁武帝 (464 年—549 年), 名萧衍, 汉相萧何第
二十五代世孙, 南北朝时期梁朝政权的建立者, 在位时间
达四十八年之久。

⑦ 侯景 (503 年—552 年), 原为东魏大将, 于梁武帝太
清元年 (547 年) 率部投降梁朝, 驻守寿阳, 但不久起兵
反叛, 于三年 (549 年) 攻破建康, 致使梁武帝被困饿死
城中。

【今文解译】 伍子胥决心为父兄报仇, 最后攻破了楚国都城郢; 申包胥
决心拯救楚君于危难之中, 结果保全了楚国。由此可以看
出, 人只要有决心, 事情都是能够办到的。

秦始皇灭掉东周的那一年, 正是后来推翻秦王朝的刘邦
刚刚诞生的时候; 梁武帝灭南齐的那一年, 正是后来起
兵破梁都城的侯景率部投梁的时候。此所谓天道好还。

【English Translation】

Wu Zixu* vowed to avenge his father and elder brother, and therefore ruined
Ying, the capital of Chu. On the other hand, Shen Baoxu* was determined to
save the king and then succeeded in protecting the state from being destroyed.
From this we see that the will of a true man can always be counted on.

The year the First Emperor of Qin* dismantled the Eastern Zhou is the time
Liu Bang* was just born, who overthrew the Qin Empire afterwards. The year
Emperor Wu of Liang* eliminated Southern Qi is the time Hou Jing* gave in
his submission to Liang, who sent the Liang Dynasty to tomb subsequently.
From this we know that heavenly retribution, good or bad, is bound to come in
turn.

【English Annotation】

* Wu Zixu (?-484BC), named Wu Yuan, general and prime minister of the
state of Wu during the late Spring and Autumn Period, well versed in military
and political strategies.
* Shen Baoxu(?-?), a senior official of the state of Chu during the Spring and
Autumn Period (770BC-476BC). When Wu Zixu, for the purpose to revenge

his father and elder brother who was killed by Emperor Ping of Chu, led the troops of Wu in person to attack Chu in 506BC, Shen, once the good friend of Wu Zixu's, went to Qin and requested military assistance. Attacked by the troops of Wu and Qin from both sides, Wu Zixu had to issue the order to withdraw. When the state was secured, Emperor Zhao of Chu intended to award Shen, but he declined and retreated forever.

* The First Emperor of Qin (259BC-210BC), named Ying Zheng or Zhao Zheng, founder of the Qin Empire, who accomplished the unification of China in 221BC (the 26th year of his reign), hence esteemed as the greatest politician, strategist and military commander in the Chinese feudal history.

(Special note: According to historical records, the Eastern Zhou was dismantled by King Zhuangxiang of Qin in 249BC instead of the First Emperor, who was then only ten years old.)

* Liu Bang (256BC-195BC), Emperor Gao, founder of the Han Dynasty (r. 202BC-195BC), usually called the Lord of Pei before assuming the throne.

* Emperor Wu of Liang (464-549), named Xiao Yan and styled Shuda, founder (r. 502BC-549) of the Liang Dynasty of the Southern Dynasties.

* Hou Jing (503-552), a general of the Eastern Wei during the Southern Dynasties, who surrendered to Emperor Wu of Liang in 547 but rebelled against the emperor very soon and forced him to die of hunger in 549.

14. 有才者如浑金璞玉　为学者如行云流水

14. A talented man should be like unrefined gold and uncut jade and like flowing water and floating cloud, the man of learning.

　　有才必韬藏，如浑金璞玉，暗然而日章也。为学无间断，如流水行云，日进而不已也。

【今文解译】　　一个人的才能应该隐藏起来，要像未加冶炼的金子和未经琢磨的玉石，渐渐彰显自己的光芒。

　　　　　　　　一个人做学问切不可时断时续，而应像奔腾的流水和飘浮的行云，每天都要有所收获和进步。

【English Translation】

A talented man should hide his talents by keeping it as unrefined gold and uncut jade, and only in this way can his talents be increasing from time to time without being noticed.

The man of learning must ceaselessly persist in his own endeavor by doing it like flowing water and floating cloud, and only in this way can progress be made each day.

15. 积善有余庆　积财易遗祸

15. The accumulation of goodness brings about good fortune while the accumulation of wealth invites calamity.

积善之家，必有余庆；积不善之家，必有余殃。可知积善以遗子孙，其谋甚远也。

贤而多财，则损其志；愚而多财，则益其过。可知积财以遗子孙，其害无穷也。

【今文解译】　如果一个家庭多多行善，那么他们的子孙一定会有连绵不断的福祉；如果一个家庭常常作恶，那么他们的后代一定会遭到无休无止的灾祸。由此可知，把家庭的善德留传给子孙是一种目光长远的行为。
一个原本贤能的人如果拥有很多钱财，这些钱财只会削弱他的意志；一个原本愚昧的人如果拥有很多钱财，这些钱财只会加重他的愚昧。由此可知，把家庭积聚的财富遗传给子孙是一种危害无穷的做法。

【English Translation】

If a family has granted a lot of benevolence to others, its descendants will have boundless good fortune. If it has done any malevolence to others, its descendants will be afflicted with endless misfortune. From this we know that it is a long-term consideration for a family to bless its descendants by accumulating benevolence.

If you are wise yet rich at the same time, the riches you have might impair your will. If you are stupid yet rich at the same time, the riches you have might increase your folly. From this we realize that it is an endless misfortune for a family to benefit its descendants with a legacy of accumulated wealth.

16. 要以德化人　勿以财累己

16. Influence others with virtue and don't let your wealth weigh you down.

　　每见待子弟，严厉者易至成德，姑息者多有败行，则父兄之教育所系也；又见有子弟，聪颖者忽入下流，庸愚者转为上达，则父兄之培植所关也。人品之不高，总为一利字看不破；学业之不进，总为一懒字丢不开。德足以感人，而以有德当大权，其感尤速；财足以累己，而以有财处乱世，其累尤深。

【今文解译】　　每每能看到这样的情形：对子孙要求严格的，可使他们养成良好的品行，而对子孙姑息纵容的，往往使他们道德败坏，这都和接受父兄什么样的教育是密不可分的。还能看到另一种情形：一些原本十分聪慧的子孙突然变得低俗起来，而原本十分平庸的子孙却明显变得人品高贵起来，这同样都和接受父兄什么样的熏陶是密不可分的。

　　人品低下，都是因为看不破一个利字；学业没有进步，都是由于丢不开一个懒字。

　　良好的品德足可感化人，如果感化者既有良好的品德又有显赫的声誉和地位，那么他感化人的作用就会尤其明显。

　　财富足可拖累人的心力，如果拥有很多财富且又恰逢多事之秋，那么财富对人的拖累就愈加厉害。

【English Translation】

It has been very often that children who are taught with strictness become well cultivated and those who are treated over-tolerantly fall into evil ways. It's all up to the education they have received from the adults of their families.

It has also been very often that some of the smart children unexpectedly become degenerated and some of the mediocre ones become heads and shoulders above others. Again, it's all up to the influence they have had from the adults of their families.

Sinking in low personality, it's always because that one fails to see through the word of profit. Lagging behind in study, it's normally because that one fails to cast away the word of laziness.

It's easy to influence people with righteousness, and more so if done by a person who is marked with fame and rank.

It's burdensome to have too much wealth, and more so when in troubled times.

17. 读书无论资性高低　立身不嫌家世贫贱

17. Aptitude is not a decisive factor in study; poor family status does not affect personal establishment.

　　读书无论资性①高低，但能勤学好问，凡事思一个所以然，自有义理贯通之日。立身②不嫌家世贫贱，但能忠厚老成，所行无一毫苟且处，便为乡党仰望之人。

【中文注释】　　① 资性：天资，天分，悟性。
　　　　　　　　② 立身：为人处事。

【今文解译】　　读书不论天资高低，只要勤学好问，凡事都探个究竟，自会有明白其中含义和道理的那一天。
　　　　　　　　立身无关家世贫贱，只要忠厚老实，从来不做有失体统的事情，就一定会成为众所敬仰的人。

【English Translation】

Human intelligence is not a factor so decisive in study. As long as you can learn and consult unceasingly, and probe into the whys and wherefores of difficult points, there must be a day when you penetrate the meaning and reasons in the books.

Poor family status is not a thing so important for gaining a place in society. As long as you can behave yourself in a way of honesty and kindheartedness, and do nothing against public ethics, you will surely be a person respected by all the surrounding people.

18. 恶乡愿　弃鄙夫

18. Stay away from hypocrites and despise vulgarians.

孔子何以恶乡愿^①，只为他似忠似廉，无非假面孔^②；孔子何以弃鄙夫^③，只因他患得患失，尽是俗心肠^④。

【中文注释】　① 恶乡愿：恶，讨厌、厌恶；乡愿，貌似忠诚老实、实质欺世盗名的人。
② 假面孔：伪善的嘴脸；具有欺骗性。
③ 弃鄙夫：弃，厌弃，瞧不起；鄙夫，小人。
④ 俗心肠：此处指唯利是图者。

【今文解译】　孔子为什么厌恶伪君子? 就是因为他们看似忠厚老实，其实是一副虚假伪善的嘴脸。
孔子为什么鄙视世俗小人? 就是因为他们太患得患失，全然是一副唯利是图的心肠。

【English Translation】

The reason why Confucius disliked the ones seemingly honest and upright is that they are hypocritical and deceitful.
The reason why Confucius despised the mean fellows is that they are the vulgarians who only care about their own interests.

19. 精明败家风　朴实振家业

19. Too much astuteness in social dealings ruins family reputation; plainness and honesty revitalize family businesses.

　　打算精明，自谓得计，然败祖父之家声者，必此人也；朴实浑厚，初无甚奇，然培子孙之元气者，必此人也。

【今文解译】　　算计十分精明，得逞后便暗自窃喜，然而败坏家庭祖传名声的，必定是这种人。
　　　　　　　　为人忠厚老实，初看平淡无奇，然而能培养出子孙质朴品质的，必定是这种人。

【English Translation】

He who is about to ruin the family's fame his ancestors have established must be the one who is too astute in social relationship and self-complacent when he has his way.

He who can cultivate his sons and grandsons into unsophisticated men must be the one who is simple and honest and persists on doing so even if there is little effect in the beginning.

20. 明辨是非　不忘廉耻

20. To be a man, one should distinguish right from wrong and keep in his heart the sense of shame.

心能辨是非，处事方能决断；人不忘廉耻，立身自不卑污①。

【中文注释】　① 自不卑污：自然不会自甘堕落。

【今文解译】　心中有了正确的是非观，处理起事情来就能做到果断坚决。

做人不忘廉耻，为人处世就自然不会做出有损品格的事来。

【English Translation】

Only when a man has cultivated the ability to distinguish between right and wrong can he handle affairs with resolution.

Only when a man has kept in his heart the sense of shame can he conduct himself in a way free of filth and mire.

21. 愚忠愚孝不可取　假仁假义要不得

21. Neither foolish loyalty and filial piety nor sham benevolence and righteousness are advisable.

忠有愚忠，孝有愚孝，可知忠孝二字不是伶俐人做得来；仁有假仁，义有假义，可知仁义两途不无奸恶人藏其内。

【今文解译】　忠有冥顽愚昧的忠，孝有冥顽愚昧的孝。从中可以知道，真正的忠和孝不一定是那些八面玲珑的人可以做得到的。

仁有假模假样的仁，义有假模假样的义。从中可以知道，在讲求仁义的人群里，未必没有奸佞邪恶的人混迹其中。

【English Translation】

There is loyalty which is called foolish loyalty and filial piety called foolish filial piety. These are the two moral entities that no smart guys can afford to go with.

There is benevolence which is called sham benevolence and righteousness called sham righteousness. These are the two paths in which the wicked ones hide themselves.

22. 权势如烟云过眼　奸邪无事生非

22. Power and influence are floating clouds; an evil man makes trouble out of nothing.

　　权势之徒，虽至亲亦作威福，岂知烟云过眼，已立见其消亡；奸邪之辈，即平地亦起风波，岂知神鬼有灵，不肯听其颠倒。

【今文解译】　拥有权势的人即使对身边最亲近的人也作威作福，殊不知手中的权势只不过是转眼即逝的烟云而已。
　　　　　　　奸诈邪恶的人即使没事也会惹是生非，殊不知神鬼其实也是有灵魂感知的，不会任凭他们胡作非为。

【English Translation】

The man of power and influence even lord it over his kinsfolk, unaware that the power and influence he possesses now are only the smokes and clouds which will disappear at any time.

A crafty, evil man even makes trouble out of nothing, not knowing that the ghosts and spirits are all sharp-eyed enough to perceive his scheme and will not let him run wild willfully.

23. 不为富贵所动　常将忠孝记挂

23. Never be moved by wealth and rank and always keep in mind loyalty and filiality.

　　自家富贵，不着意里；人家富贵，不着眼里。此是何等胸襟^①！古人忠孝，不离心头；今人忠孝，不离口头。此是何等志量^②！

【中文注释】　　① 胸襟：胸怀和气度。
　　　　　　　　② 志量：志气和度量。

【今文解译】　　自己家里富贵了全然无意炫耀，别人家里富贵了连看都不看一眼。这是何等的胸襟！
　　　　　　　　古人把"忠孝"二字牢记在心里，而今人常把"忠孝"二字四处传扬。这是何等的志量！

【English Translation】

That one does not think too much of the wealth and rank one's own family has, nor take a glance at the wealth and rank other families have — what a free and unaffected deportment!

That people of old time always kept in mind the principles of loyalty and filiality, and people of present time often talk about the principles of loyalty and filiality — what a great inspiration!

24. 物命可惜　人心可回

24. Lives of the all living beings under heaven are worth cherishing.

　　王者不令人放生，而无故却不杀生，则物命可惜也；圣人不责人无过，唯多方诱之改过，庶人心可回也。

【今文解译】　君王虽然从来不下命令让人去放生，却也不会无缘无故地滥杀无辜。这是因为天下的生灵都是值得珍爱的。
圣人不要求人没有过错，但会通过各种方式去引导他们改正过错。这是因为大部分犯错的人都愿回心转意的。

【English Translation】

Princes would not execute living beings for no reason though they have never issued orders to release captives. This is because that all the lives of the living beings under heaven are worth cherishing.

Sages would never demand people free of errors but would rather persuade them to correct their errors if any. This is because that most of those who have made errors are willing to correct them.

25. 处事论是非　立言贵精详

25. In handling affairs, one should be clear about right and wrong, and attentive to intensiveness and thoroughness in writing and speaking.

大丈夫^①处事，论是非不论祸福；士君子^②立言，贵平正尤贵精详^③。

【中文注释】　① 大丈夫：有志气的男子；男子汉。

② 士君子：读书人；知识分子。

③ 精详：精当详尽。

【今文解译】　有为之士为人处事时，只关心正确与否而不关心给他带来的是灾祸还是福祉。

有学之士发表言论或写文章时，重要的是公平公正但更重要的是论述要精辟。

【English Translation】

In handling affairs, a true man only cares about what is right and wrong, not about whether the affairs will turn out to be a good fortune to him or not.

In writing or speaking, a knightly scholar first pays attention to justice and equity, and then more attention to the intensiveness and thoroughness.

26. 有科名心　无济世才

26. There are some who only have the heart to gain scholarship but no ability to govern and serve.

存科名之心者，未必有琴书之乐；讲性命之学者，不可无经济之才。

【今文解译】　一心想博取科举功名的人，未必能体会琴棋书画的兴趣。
讲求生命形而上境界的学者，不能没有经世济民的才能。

【English Translation】

He who is absorbed in scholarly honor and official rank may not appreciate his interest in scholars' four fancies*.
He who seeks to transcend the earthly world should never be deprived of the ability to serve the country and the people.

【English Annotation】

* Scholars' four fancies are referred to lute-playing, chess, calligraphy and painting.

27. 静而止闹　淡而消窘

27. Motionlessness can calm down disturbance while plainness can avoid embarrassment.

　　泼妇之啼哭怒骂，伎俩要亦无多，唯静而镇之，则自止矣。谗人之簸弄挑唆，情形虽若甚迫，苟淡而置之，是自消矣。

【今文解译】　　泼妇啼哭怒骂，无理取闹，可以玩的把戏也就这些。只要不予理会，她就会自知无趣，停止哭闹了。

　　　　　　　搬弄是非的人造谣中伤，挑拨离间，情形着实令人难堪。但如能泰然处之，谣言也就不攻自破了。

【English Translation】

Wanton tricks of a shrew, such as crying and cursing, are few, if any; so long as you keep her down by doing nothing, she will stop her wildness herself. Discord brought about by the slanderous might be really embarrassing; but if you handle it with perfect composure the discord will subside itself.

28. 行善救人　脱身俗情

28. Be willing to help others and one will break away from poor taste.

肯救人坑坎中，便是活菩萨^①；能脱身牢笼外，便是大英雄。

【中文注释】　① 活菩萨：指具有慈悲与觉了之心、能救渡众生于苦难迷惑、并引导众生成佛的人。常比作"大善人"或"大恩人"。

【今文解译】　肯把人从危难与困苦中解救出来的人，就是活菩萨。
　　　　　　能从世俗的桎梏与羁绊摆脱出来的人，就是真英雄。

【English Translation】

He that is willing to lend a merciful hand to the suffering and the needy is a living Buddha.
He that is capable to extricate himself from the fetters of this mundane world is a true hero.

29. 气性乖张短命　言语尖刻薄福

29. Those who are eccentric and often behave in a queer way are short of longevity and luck.

气性乖张，多是天亡之子；语言尖刻，终为薄福之人。

【今文解译】　脾气性格乖张暴躁的人，大多寿命不长。
　　　　　　　动辄出言尖酸刻薄的人，一般福分较浅。

【English Translation】

Those who are eccentric and often behave in a queer way are mostly short-lived.

Those who talk in an acrimonious tone at every turn are normally less blessed.

30. 胸怀大志　脚踏实地

30. We should not only be ambitious, but also down-to-earth.

　　志不可不高，志不高则同流合污，无足有为矣；心不可太大，心太大则舍近图远，难期有成矣。

【今文解译】　　一个人的志趣不可不高雅，志趣不高雅，就一定会与世俗庸劣之辈同流合污，结果一定难有作为。

　　　　　　　　一个人的心气不可太大，心气太大，就一定会舍弃眼前的目标而好高骛远，到头来必定一事无成。

【English Translation】

A man's inclination should be noble and elegant, or he will be lightly inflicted with bad influence and thus become good for nothing in the end.

A man's intention should not be too lofty and unrealistic, or he will forgo what is close at hand and seek what is far afield, and finally get nowhere.

31. 贫贱不能移　富贵要济世

31. Remain unyielding when poor; be useful to the world when rich.

　　贫贱非辱，贫贱而谄求于人者为辱；富贵非荣，富贵而利济于世者为荣。讲大经纶①，只是实实落落；有真学问，决不怪怪奇奇。

【中文注释】　　① 大经纶：经纶，本意为经过整理的蚕丝。此处喻规划、管理政治的才能。大经纶也即满腹经纶之意。

【今文解译】　　贫贱不是耻辱，但因为贫贱而去低三下四地乞求别人，这才是耻辱。
富贵不是荣耀，但富贵的同时还能慷慨解囊救助世人，这才是荣耀。
满腹经纶的人，只有奉献出自己的聪明才智才名副其实。
真正有知识和学问的人，绝对不会装模作样、故弄玄虚。

【English Translation】

It's not a shame to be poor and humble, but so indeed if one has resort to others in a way of degrading oneself because of poverty and humbleness.

It's not an honor to be wealthy and influential, but so indeed if one does something good and useful to the world with the wealth and influence of his own.

A man full of wisdom and ability can only be so called when he earnestly dedicates what he has in mind.

A man who is really well versed in knowledge and learning will never behave in a queer way.

32. 即物穷理　名副其实

32. To derive the implications from the name of a subject is always advisable.

古人比父子为桥梓^①，比兄弟为花萼，比朋友为芝兰，敦伦者，当即物穷理也；今人称诸生曰秀才，称贡生曰明经，称举人曰孝廉^②，为士者，当顾名思义也。

【中文注释】　① 桥梓：也即乔梓。乔的树干高大，梓的树干低矮，古人常将它们比作父与子。

② 秀才、明经、孝廉：皆为明清时人们对考取这三个不同科举功名的学生的敬称。秀才是明清两代对生员的通称，传承自汉朝，别称茂才，原指才之秀者，始见于《管子·小匡篇》；明经是一种官员举荐遴选科目，因被举荐者须明习经学，故以"明经"为名，始于汉武帝时期，至宋神宗时期被废除；孝廉是汉武帝时设立的察举和任用官员的一种考试科目，是"孝顺亲长、廉能正直"的意思，明清两代以"孝廉"这个称呼用作对举人的雅称。

【今文解译】　古人把父子关系比作乔木与梓木，把兄弟关系比作花瓣与花萼，把朋友关系比作芝草与兰花。讲究人伦大统的人，应当学会通过对事物的观察来类比人与人之间的关系并加以善待。

今人称通过县级考试的读书人为秀才，称被地方官推荐进入太学的读书人为明经，称在省级考试中榜上有名的读书人为孝廉。有志于学的人，应当明白这些称谓的含义并好自为之。

【English Translation】

In ancient time, people used to compare the relationship between father and son to arbor and catalpa, that between brothers to petals and sepals of a flower, and that between friends to iris and orchard. Whoever pays attention to the natural bonds and ethical principles should try his best to learn to treat them well by analogizing the substance to the significance humanly related through thorough observation.

While at present time, people take a habit of calling the students who have passed the examination at the county level as *xiucai*, the scholars recommended by local prefectures or county governments as *mingjing*, the successful candidates in the imperial examination at the provincial level as *xiaolian*. Whoever is interested in learning should know clearly what these titles imply and look out for himself.

33. 以身作则　心平气和

33. In daily life, we must make ourselves an example and be gentle with others.

父兄有善行，子弟学之或不肖；父兄有恶行，子弟学之则无不肖。可知父兄教子弟，必正其身以率之，无庸徒事言词也。

君子有过行，小人嫉之不能容；君子无过行，小人嫉之亦不能容。可知君子处小人，必平其气以待之，不可稍形激切也。

【今文解译】　父辈或兄长们有好的行为，子弟后辈们即使学了也不一定像；而父辈或兄长们有坏的行为，子弟后辈们学了就没有不像的。由此我们可知，父辈兄长们教育子弟后辈们，一定先要端正自己的行为以作表率，不能尽说些无用的空话。

君子如果有过失，小人一定会因为妒忌而趁机进行人身攻击；君子即使没有过失，小人也会出于妒忌而横加毁谤。由此我们得知，君子与小人相处时，一定要心平气和来对待，切不可在言行上有半点急躁的情绪，以免激怒小人。

【English Translation】

When the elder ones of a family have done something good, the younger ones would follow them though not much alike at length; but when they have done something bad, the younger ones would also imitate them and do it lifelike. It is from this we know that before training the younger ones, the elder ones should first rectify themselves and set a good example for them, rather than do it merely with empty talk.

When the man of virtue has done something wrong, the base man would attack him and never let him go. Even if the man of virtue has done nothing wrong, the base man would also like to defile him and not let him go lightly. It is from this we know that when dealing with base men, the man of virtue should smooth their temperaments and avoid being attacked by them out of his own radical deeds and words.

34. 不贻羞于父母　勿贻害于子孙

34. Don't do anything stupid to shame your parents and injure your offspring.

守身不敢妄为，恐贻羞于父母；创业还须深虑，恐贻害于子孙。

【今文解译】　谨守自己的操行不敢轻举妄动，是因为害怕自己的行为不够谨慎而使父母蒙羞。
创立自己的事业之前深思熟虑，是因为害怕自己的计划不够周全而贻害子孙。

【English Translation】

In order not to leave a legacy of shame to his parents, one should avoid acting rashly in personal behavior.
When starting a venture, one should deliberate carefully for fear of involving his offspring into trouble.

35. 待人不可势利　习业万勿粗心

35. Don't be snobbish in dealing with others; don't be careless in doing things.

无论做何等人，总不可有势利气；无论习何等业，总不可有粗浮心。

【今文解译】 不论你是什么样的人，都不能以势利的眼光看待社会上的人和事。

不论你从事什么样的职业，都不能有轻慢浮躁、万事不屑的心态。

【English Translation】

Whosoever you are should not be tainted with snobbish attitude.

Whatsoever you do should not be done in a gruff and impetuous manner.

36. 不妄自尊大　要奋发图强

36. Strive to be strong, not arrogant.

知道自家是何等身分，则不敢虚骄矣；想到他日是那样下场，则可以发愤矣。

【今文解译】　知道自己有怎样的地位和能力，就不会盲目地自视太高。想到如今的慵懒会造成将来的穷困潦倒，自当发奋努力。

【English Translation】

Knowing the status and ability you have on your part would help to warn you not to think too much of yourself.

Pondering the tragic ending you might have someday when you slack off would help to drive you to work harder.

37. 东山可再起 江心补漏迟

37. Failure can make a comeback.

常人突遭祸患，可决其再兴，心动于警励也；大家渐及消亡，难期其复振，势成于因循也。

【今文解译】 一个平常普通的人即使遭受到突如其来的祸患，仍可指望他能东山再起。这是因为他平素就具备了迎击挑战的警惕性和勇气。

一个已经成名成家的人一旦面临灭顶之灾，就很难指望他会再次振作起来。这是因为他已经养成了保守的习惯，丧失了锐气。

【English Translation】

Ordinary people are enabled to recover from a sudden disaster. This is because they have always been of vigilance and courage to meet any possible challenges head-on.

People with established reputations can hardly be expected to change the situation when approaching a fatal crisis. This is because they have become conservative for too long a time.

38. 生命有穷期　学问无止境

38. Life must have its end while knowledge has no limit.

天地无穷期，生命则有穷期，去一日，便少一日；富贵有定数，学问则无定数，求一分，便得一分。

【今文解译】　宇宙天地没有穷尽的时候，但生命却是有尽头的：过一天，生命就减少一天。

富贵是有极限的，但学问知识却没有：你多努力探求一点，就会多得到一点。

【English Translation】

The heaven and earth are inexhaustible while life is exhaustible: A day spent is a day missing.

Riches and honor have limit while knowledge has no limit: The more you learn the more you gain.

39. 做事要问心无愧　创业需量力而行

39. Things need to be done with a clear conscience; Entrepreneurship needs to be done according to one's ability.

处事有何定凭，但求此心过得去；立业无论大小，总要此身做得来。

【今文解译】　做事没有一定的标准，只要问心无愧即可。
立业不论是大还是小，只要力所能及就好。

【English Translation】

It's not a matter whether there are any set rules in dealing with affairs, but a matter that you feel no qualms upon self-examination.

It's not important whether the entrepreneurship you start is big or small, but important that you are doing what you can by yourself.

40. 气性乖张无足取 言语矫饰属可疑

40. It is undesirable to be eccentric and questionable.

气性不和平，则文章事功，俱无足取；语言多矫饰，则人品心术，尽属可疑。

【今文解译】 一个人处世不能心平气和，那么无论是学术上的成就还是社会上的功绩都不值得称道。

一个人的言辞总是矫揉造作，华而不实，那么无论他的人品还是他的心性都值得怀疑。

【English Translation】

If a man always resents the way of the world, then both his academic achievements and social merits will count for nothing.

If a man often gives his utterances in a hypocritical way, then both his moral standing and temperament will be questionable.

41. 守拙可取　交友宜慎

41. It' quite advisable to remain free from ambition and careful in making friends.

误用聪明，何若一生守拙；滥交朋友，不如终日读书。

【今文解译】　与其把聪明才智用在不该用的地方，还不如一辈子都保持笨拙。

与其不加选择地到处结交朋友，还不如整日呆在家里发奋读书。

【English Translation】

To apply intelligence at the wrong time in the wrong place is not as good as to stay in dullness for life.

To make friends without choice is not as good as to be engrossed in book-reading all day long.

42. 放眼读书　立跟做人

42. Be open-minded when reading; stand firm to be a man.

看书须放开眼孔，做人要立定脚跟。

【今文解译】　读书需要放开眼界，打开心胸。
　　　　　　　做人必须站稳立场，把握原则。

【English Translation】

When reading, one should open his mind as wide as possible.
To be a man, one should get his foothold as firm as possible.

43. 持身贵严　处世贵谦

43. Solemnness is valuable in conducting oneself, so is modesty in dealing with the world.

严近乎矜，然严是正气，矜是乖气。故持身贵严，而不可矜。

谦似乎谄，然谦是虚心，谄是媚心。故处世贵谦，而不可谄。

【今文解译】　严肃看起来有点像傲慢，然而严肃是一种浩然的正气，而傲慢则是一种乖僻的戾气，因此，持身要严肃而不可傲慢。

谦逊看起来有点像谄谀，但是谦逊是一种虚心的恭谨，而谄谀则是一种迎合的媚态，因此，处世要谦逊而不可谄谀。

【English Translation】

Solemnness and conceit are sometimes nearly of the same meaning. But actually, the former is signified as being serious in manner, while the latter as performing excessive pride in oneself. Therefore, we learn that what values in conducting ourselves is solemnness rather than conceit.

Modesty and flattery are seemingly related to each other. But in fact, the former is defined as giving priority to a person out of courtesy or consideration, and the latter as toadying to someone in a servile manner. Therefore, in dealing with the world, we'd better be of modesty rather than flattery.

44. 善用其财　无愧其禄

44. It will bring you no shame if you can make a good use of your salary.

　　财不患其不得，患财得而不能善用其财；禄不患其不来，患禄来而不能无愧其禄。

【今文解译】　不必担心得不到钱财，而应担心得到了钱财却不能合理地使用钱财。
　　　　　　　不必担心领不到俸禄，而应担心领取了俸禄却做不到无愧于这份俸禄。

【English Translation】

It is not a worry to slip the chance to make money, but a worry to misuse the money when gained.
It is not a fear to fail to get the official's salary, but a fear to be not equal to the salary when given.

45. 交益友　立品行

45. It's better to make helpful friends and behave yourself properly.

　　交朋友增体面，不如交朋友益身心；教子弟求显荣，不如教子弟立品行。

【今文解译】　　与其为了争面子而去交朋友，不如结交一些对自己身心俱益的朋友。

与其教导学生去追求显达荣耀，不如教导他们树立高尚美好的品德。

【English Translation】

To make friends for the sake of face is no better than to make friends for the good of the body and heart.

To instruct our disciples to seek glory is no better than to instruct them to set up moral standards.

46. 君子如神　小人如鬼

46. The man of virtue is like a deity and a ghost, the man of no virtue.

　　君子存心，但凭忠信，而妇孺皆敬之如神，所以君子乐得为君子；

小人处世，尽设机关，而乡党皆避之若鬼，所以小人枉做了小人。

【今文解译】　君子的心里装着忠厚与诚信，妇女儿童敬他们如同敬神一般，因而，君子都一个个很乐意被称作君子。

　　　　　　　小人总是处心积虑地玩花招，老百姓都把他们当恶鬼躲避，因而，小人机关算尽，到了也还是徒劳。

【English Translation】

The man of virtue always bears in mind the concepts of honesty and credibility and therefore is esteemed by women and children as a deity. That's why the man of virtue would like to be so called.

The man of little virtue spares no effort to play tricks in doing things and therefore is kept at a distance by the locals and treated as a devil. Eventually, all the tricks he schemes can only end in vain.

47. 严以律己 宽以待人

47. Be strict with yourself and lenient with others.

求个良心管我，留些余地处人。

【今文解译】 做人，必须要有一颗良心来约束自己。

处世，必须留有一些余地来宽容别人。

【English Translation】

Let your conscience be the inspector of your behaviors.
Leave some leeway in getting along with fellow beings.

48. 守口如瓶　持身若璧

48. Keep your mouth as tight as a bottle and be yourself as pure as jade.

　　一言足以召大祸，故古人守口如瓶，惟恐其覆坠也；一行足以玷终身，故古人饬躬若璧，惟恐有瑕疵也。

【今文解译】　　一句不慎的言辞就足以招来大祸，所以古人都习惯于守口如瓶，唯恐失言导致万劫不复的后果。

　　　　　　　　一个不慎的举动就足以使自己蒙羞一辈子，所以古人都讲究守身如玉，唯恐不谨慎而遗憾终生。

【English Translation】

An imprudent word is enough to invite a fatal disaster, so the ancient people were all cautious with their words, for fear that a casual word would send them to their dooms eternally.

An imprudent deed is enough to cause a lifelong disgrace for a man, so the ancient people always kept themselves as pure as jade, for fear that a careless deed might bring a lifelong regret.

49. 不较横逆　安守贫穷

49. Overlook the importunate persons and be content with poverty.

　　颜子①之不较，孟子之自反，是贤人处横逆之方；子贡②之无谄，原思③之坐弦，是贤人守贫穷之法。

【中文注释】　① 颜子：即孔门弟子颜回，字子渊，十四岁拜孔子为师，是孔门"十哲"之首，谦虚好学，宅民仁厚。后世有"复圣"之称。
　　　　　　② 子贡：即孔门弟子端木赐，孔门"十哲"之一，善于雄辩，办事通达。后世有"先贤端木子"之称。
　　　　　　③ 原思：即孔门弟子原宪，字子思，孔门"七十二贤"之一，清静守节，安贫乐道。

【今文解译】　有人胡搅蛮缠时，颜渊不予计较，而孟轲则反躬自省。这是贤者对待胡搅蛮缠者的做法。
　　　　　　面对贫穷，子贡不屑卑躬屈膝，原思只是兀自坐地弹琴。这是贤者对待贫穷的自处之道。

【English Translation】

Whenever there occurred something rude and unreasonable, Yan Yuan* would bear patiently and Mencius* would only take it for self-examination. What the two played is the way of a sage in dealing with such things.

Whenever low in abject poverty, Zi Gong* would never go crawling to anyone and Yuan Si* would just sit on the ground playing the strings. What the two performed is the method sages apply in coping with poverty.

【English Annotation】

* Yan Yuan (521BC-481BC), styled Ziyuan, one of the ten best disciples of Confucius, also known as Yan Hui or Yan Zi.
* Mencius (c. 372BC-289BC), given name Ke and styled Ziyu, a thinker, educationist and representative figure of Confucianism during the Warring

States Period.

* Zi Gong (520BC-456BC), named Duanmu Ci, one of the ten best disciples of Confucius, a politician and merchant good at speech and eloquence, and prime minister of the states of Lu and Wei in succession, who spent six years on keeping beside the grave of Confucius and thus won high respect from the contemporaries and later generations.

* Yuan Si (515BC-? BC), also named Yuan Xian and styled Zi Si, one of the seventy-two sage disciples of Confucius.

50. 白云山岳皆文章　黄花松柏乃吾师

50. White clouds and high mountains are all good texts; chrysanthemums and pines are my examples.

　　观朱霞悟其明丽，观白云悟其卷舒，观山岳悟其灵奇，观河海悟其浩瀚，则俯仰间皆文章也。对绿竹得其虚心，对黄华得其晚节，对松柏得其本性，对芝兰得其幽芳，则游览处皆师友也。

【今文解译】　　观赏赤红的彩霞就能领略到它的明亮美丽，观赏雪白的浮云就能领略到它的时聚时散，观赏高耸的峻岭就能领略到它的空灵奇特，观赏浩瀚的河海就能领略到它的波澜壮阔。只要有一颗能观善察的心，俯仰之间就都能领略到美的神韵。
　　　　　　　　端详翠竹可以品赏到它的虚心谦卑，端详菊花可以品赏到它的高风亮节，端详松柏可以品赏到它的坚韧不屈，端详芝草兰花可以品赏到它的醉人幽香。游览于广袤的大自然中，你会发现身边的一草一木都仿佛是师友一般让你受益匪浅。

【English Translation】

To watch sun rays, appreciate the brightness and beauty; to watch white clouds, appreciate the massing and scattering; to watch lofty mountains, appreciate the eccentricity and peculiarity; to watch seas and rivers, appreciate the boundlessness and extensiveness. So long as one has an understanding heart, whatever one watches will soon be full of texture.

When confronted with a green bamboo, taste the modesty of it; when confronted with a yellow chrysanthemum, taste the lasting integrity of it; when confronted with a pine tree, taste the constancy of it; when confronted with an iris or an orchard, taste the delicate fragrance of it. So long as one has the will to taste, whatever one comes upon and observes will be tasteful.

51. 行善自乐　奸谋自坏

51. The person who is willing to help others entertains himself; the fellow who hatches a plot can be ruined by his own plot.

　　行善济人，人遂得以安全，即在我亦为快意；逞奸谋事，事难必其稳便，可惜他徒自坏心。

【今文解译】　做好事帮助别人，被帮助的人会因我而得到解脱，而我自己心里也因此充满了快乐。

做好事帮助别人，被帮助的人会因我而得到解脱，而我自己心里也因此充满了快乐。

使奸诈算计别人，结果未必就能如愿以偿，可惜奸诈小人却白白玷污了自己的良知。

【English Translation】

When a person has done something to help others, others thereupon are secured; this alone makes the person deserve a happy celebration.

When a person hatches a plot against a thing, the thing may not come off as bad as hatched, but the person has really blotted out his conscience.

52. 以人为镜　防微杜渐

52. To practice precaution, take human as mirror.

　　不镜于水，而镜于人，则吉凶可鉴也；不蹶于山，而蹶于垤，则细微宜防也。

【今文解译】　不以水为镜，而以别人的经验教训为镜，这样就可以明察吉凶福祸。
没跌倒在大山上，却跌倒在土堆上，这证明小事情也不能掉以轻心。

【English Translation】

Take your reflection in man rather than in water, and you will be enabled to discriminate good luck from bad.

People are liable to stumble over a hillock rather than a hill; this shows that small things can't be taken lightly.

53. 谨守规模　必无大错

53. Act according to the public conventions and one will make no big mistake.

凡事谨守规模，必无大错；一生但足衣食，便称小康。

【今文解译】　做事谨遵公认的规则秩序，就一定不会犯大的错。
一辈子不愁穿不愁吃，就一定称得上是小康生活。

【English Translation】

Act according to the public conventions and one will make no big mistake.
A lifetime of ample food and clothing is what termed a well-to-do life.

54. 耐得住烦　吃得起亏

54. Be patient in everything and ready to suffer losses at any time.

十分不耐烦，乃为人大病；一味学吃亏，是处事良方。

【今文解译】　做什么事都没有耐心，是一个人很大的缺点。
随时都准备吃点亏，是为人处世最好的方法。

【English Translation】

Being extremely impatient in anything is a serious failing in conducting oneself.

Being ready to suffer losses at any time is a good way in dealing with the world.

55. 习读书业　知读书乐

55. Taking learning as a lifetime hobby, one should know the pleasure in it.

习读书之业，便当知读书之乐；存为善之心，不必邀为善之名。

【今文解译】　以读书为自己毕生爱好，就应该知道读书的乐趣。
　　　　　　　有心做善事，就不应该以行善来博取自己的名声。

【 English Translation 】

Taking learning as a lifetime hobby, one should know the pleasure in it.
Having the heart to do good to others, one needn't get oneself known to all.

56. 知己不足　学业日进

56. Only when you are aware of your shortcomings can you study hard and make progress every day.

知往日所行之非，则学日进矣；见世人可取者多，则德日进矣。

【今文解译】　只有意识到自己还有缺点和短板，学业才会日益精进。只有发现世人的可取之处那么多，德行才会不断提高。

【English Translation】

Only when you are aware of your shortcomings can you study hard and make progress every day.
Only when you know those worth learning are many can you improve your morality ceaselessly.

57. 敬人者人恒敬之　靠人者莫若靠己

57. To respect others is to respect yourself; to rely on others is no better than to rely on yourself.

敬他人，即是敬自己；靠自己，胜于靠他人。

【今文解译】　敬重别人，也即敬重自己。
依靠自己，胜于依靠别人。

【English Translation】

To respect others is to respect yourself.
Rather rely on yourself than on others.

58. 学长者助人之道　识君子修己之功

58. Learn the way of helping others from the elders and from the men of virtue, the way of moral cultivation.

见人善行，多方赞成；见人过举，多方提醒。此长者待人之道也。

闻人誉言，加意奋勉；闻人谤语，加意警惕。此君子修己之功也。

【今文解译】　看到别人行善积德就多多予以赞赏，看到别人行为失当就多多予以提醒，这是长者应有的待人之道。

听到别人的赞誉就愈加奋勉，听到别人的诋毁就愈加警醒，这是君子提高自身修为必须下的死功夫。

【English Translation】

When we see someone doing good, we'd better praise him widely. When we see someone doing wrong, we'd better warn him diligently. These are the ways the elders must take in social dealings.

When we hear someone praise us, we'd better behave even better. When we hear someone slander us, we'd better heighten our vigilance. These are the manners a gentleman must have in moral cultivation.

59. 奢侈悭吝俱可败家 庸愚精明都能覆事

59. Luxury is enough to dissipate a family, so is stinginess; stupidity is enough to spoil a thing, so is astuteness.

奢侈足以败家,悭吝亦足以败家。奢侈之败家,犹出常情;而悭吝之败家,必遭奇祸。

庸愚足以覆事,精明亦足以覆事。庸愚之覆事,犹为小咎;而精明之覆事,必见大凶。

【今文解译】 奢靡挥霍足可败家,小气吝啬也足可败家。因为奢靡挥霍而败家的,尚属情有可原;而由于小气吝啬而败家的,则必定招致飞来横祸。

愚昧笨拙足可坏事,精明算计也足可坏事。因为愚昧笨拙而坏事的,只是小过失;而由于精明算计而坏事的,则必然是凶险的大灾难。

【English Translation】

Luxury is enough to dissipate a family, so is stinginess. It's usual that luxury dissipates a family, but unusual and disastrous if stinginess does so.
Stupidity is enough to spoil a thing, so is astuteness. It's a minor penalty that stupidity spoils a thing, but a serious and dangerous one if astuteness does so.

60. 安守本业　不合浊流

60. Do your own business and never go with the turbid current.

种田人，改习尘市生涯，定为败路；读书人，干与衙门词讼，便入下流。

【今文解译】　以种田为生的人改行经商做买卖，注定是一条失败的道路。

以读书为业的人掺和衙门中的诉讼之事，一定是自处下流。

【English Translation】

A farmer who quits his old line of work and takes trading as his occupation is bound to fail at last.

A scholar who entangles himself in the lawsuits for others is sure to degrade himself sooner or later.

61. 衣食比下有余 学业比上不足

61. It's not desirable to be worse off than some in study and better off than many in daily life.

常思某人境界不及我，某人命运不及我，则可以知足矣；常思某人德业胜于我，某人学问胜于我，则可以自惭矣。

【今文解译】 时时想着别人的境遇不及我，别人的命运不如我，心里也就不会忿忿不平了。

常常想着别人的道德修养胜于我，别人的学识超过我，心里不免充满了惭愧。

【 English Translation 】

Frequently think about the living conditions someone else has inferior to ours and the fate someone else has more miserable than ours, and we will naturally be content with the lot of our own.

Frequently think about the moral achievement someone else has made superior to ours and the knowledge someone else has gained more profound than ours, and we can only be ashamed of ourselves.

62. 富不骄纵　贫不改志

62. Don't be arrogant when you are rich; don't change your mind whether you are poor.

读《论语》公子荆一章①，富者可以为法；读《论语》齐景公一章②，贫者可以自兴。舍不得钱，不能为义士；舍不得命，不能为忠臣。

【中文注释】　① 公子荆一章：即《论语·子路篇》第 8 章。全文是："子谓卫公子荆善居室，始有，曰：'苟合矣！'少有，曰：'苟完矣！'富有，曰：'苟美矣！'"（意为：卫国的公子荆善于居家理财。刚开始有一点时，他说："差不多就行了。"稍微多一点时，他说："差不多就算完备了。"更多一点时，他说："差不多算是完美了。"）孔子这段话是在赞美卫公子荆，赞美他不但知足，而且还善于治理家产。
② 齐景公一章：即《论语·季氏篇》第 12 章。全文是："齐景公有马千驷，死之日，民无德而称焉。伯夷、叔齐饿于首阳之下，民到于今称之。其斯之谓与？"（意为：齐景公有马四千匹，死的时候，百姓们觉得他没有什么德行可以称颂。伯夷、叔齐饿死在首阳山下，百姓们到现在还在称颂他们。说的就是这个意思吧。）

【今文解译】　读《论语·子路篇》第 8 章，富有的人可以此作为学习效仿的榜样；读《论语·季氏篇》第 12 章，贫穷的人可以此作为自我奋勉的动力。舍不得金钱，就成不了义士；舍不得性命，就当不了忠臣。

【English Translation】

After reading through the eighth section of the thirteenth chapter of *Analects of Confucius**, rich people will find out a good example for themselves. After reading through the twelfth section of the sixteenth chapter of *Analects of Confucius**, poor people will rise with striving spirit.
He who grudges his money cannot be a chivalrous man. He who grudges his

life cannot be a loyal subject. .

〔 English Annotation 〕

* The eighth section of the thirteenth chapter of *Analects of Confucius*: The full text of the section is as follows: Confucius talked about Duke Jing of Wei, saying, "He takes frugality as a merit with regard to a house to live in. when he first had a house, he said, 'It is more or less big enough!' Then a little more space was added to it, and he said, 'It already has everything.' When the house was further extended, he said, 'it is too sumptuous!' "
(Note: Duke Jing of Wei was a senior official of Wei. Among the ministers and other senior officials, embezzlement and extravagance were common practices. Therefore, Confucius appreciated very much Prince Jing's simple and frugal lifestyle.)
* The twelfth section of the sixteenth chapter of *Analects of Confucius*: The full text of the section is as follows: Duke Jing of Qi owned four thousand horses. When he died, the common people did not know what qualities that he possessed were worth praising. Bo Yi and Shu Qi died of hunger at the foot of Shouyang Mountains. The common people have been praising their deeds ever since.

63. 富贵要谦恭　衣禄需俭省

63. Be modest when getting rich and powerful, and frugal when carefree of food and clothing.

富贵易生祸端，必忠厚谦恭，才无大患；衣禄原有定数，必节俭简省，乃可久延。

【今文解译】　有钱又有地位容易开启祸端，所以一定要忠厚谦恭，这样才能避免大祸的发生。

家庭的收入和开销都是有定数的，所以一定要节俭度日，这样才能长久地享用。

【English Translation】

Being rich and powerful is the cause of a trouble. Only when one is honest and kind-hearted and at the same time modest and courteous, can one shun big disasters.

Household incomes and expenses are limited. Only when one unremittingly practices thrift and simplicity, can one enjoy one's good fortune as long as one wishes.

64. 作善降祥　不善降殃

64. Good luck will call on you if you show mercy while bad luck will do so if you do evil.

　　作善降祥，不善降殃，可见尘世之间，已分天堂地狱；人同此心，心同此理，可知庸愚之辈，不隔圣域贤关。

【今文解译】　一个人行善上天就会降下福祉,行恶上天就会降下祸患。由此可以发现，人世间的善恶报应其实是分毫不爽的。人的心都是相同的, 心中所想的道理也是相同的。从中可以发现，庸人和圣贤之间其实并不存在本质上的区别。

【English Translation】

Good luck will call on you if you show mercy, and bad luck will call on you if you do evil. From this we see that retribution is always distinguished so clearly without any hesitation.

Men are nearly alike in sense, and quite the same in reasons shared between them. From this we know that the mediocre and stupid and the sagacious are common to each other in nature.

65. 和平处事　正直居心

65. Live peacefully with the world and be fair and upright yourself.

和平处事，勿矫俗以为高；正直居心，勿设机以为智。

【今文解译】　要以平和的心态处理事务，不要以为刻意违背习俗就高人一筹。

要以端正耿直作为行事标准，不要以为投机取巧就比别人聪明。

【English Translation】

Live peacefully with the world, and never take it as pride to go against the social usages.

Be fair and upright, and never think highly of yourself by playing with plots.

66. 君子拯救尘世　圣贤关心民生

66. It's a duty for a man of virtue to save the world and take care about the people, for a sage.

　　君子以名教^①为乐，岂如嵇阮^②之逾闲；圣人以悲悯为心，不取沮溺^③之忘世。

【中文注释】　① 名教：指人伦之教、圣人之教，亦为儒教之别名。
　　　　　　　② 嵇阮：嵇，指嵇康；阮，指阮籍。二者皆为"竹林七贤"之一。
　　　　　　　③ 沮溺：沮，指长沮；溺，指桀溺。二者均为春秋时的隐士，与孔子是同时代人。

【今文解译】　君子皆以钻研圣人之教为乐事，怎么能像嵇康、阮籍他们那样无视正统，放任自己？
　　　　　　　圣贤无不以悲天悯人为己任，根本不屑像长沮、桀溺他们那样遗世独立，隐居一隅。

【English Translation】

A gentleman should take it as a pleasure to dig into Confucian ethical code. How can he follow the examples of Ji Kang* and Ruan Ji*, only leaving themselves out of bounds?
A sage should take it as a duty to bemoan the state of the universe and pity the fate of the mankind. How can he go and lead a reclusive life as Chang Ju and Jie Ni* did?

【English Annotation】

* Ji Kang (224-263), styled Shuye, a thinker, musician and man of letters of the Wei Kingdom during the Three Kingdoms Period, and spiritual leader of the Seven Worthies of the Bamboo Grove.
* Ruan Ji (210-263), styled Sizong, a poet, writer and thinker of the Wei Kingdom during the Three Kingdoms Period, and one of the leaders of the

Seven Worthies of the Bamboo Grove, who pursued the philosophy combining the doctrines of Taoism and Confucianism.
* Chang Ju (?-?) and Jie Ni (?-?), two hermits towards the end of the Spring and Autumn Period, contemporary with Confucius.

67. 偷安败家　争赀必伤

67. Indulgence in ease and comfort is to ruin the family; scrambling for family properties is to injure the kindred.

　　纵容子孙偷安，其后必至耽酒色而败门庭；专教子孙谋利，其后必至争赀财而伤骨肉。

【今文解译】　一味纵容子孙享受眼前的安逸，他们长大后就一定会因为沉迷酒色而败坏门庭。
　　　　　　　一心只教子孙如何敛财牟利，他们将来就一定会因为争夺财产而伤害骨肉至亲。

【English Translation】

If you connive at your kids' indulgence in ease and comfort, they will certainly be addicted to wine and women when grown up and thus corrupt your family morals at last.

If you train your kids only to rake among material wealth in favor of their own, they will most likely injure the kindred one of these days when scrambling for family properties.

68. 沉实谦恭兴业　忠厚勤俭兴家

68. Being steady and modest makes a business prosperous; being honest and diligent makes a family flourish.

　　谨守父兄教条，沉实谦恭，便是醇潜子弟；不改祖宗成法，忠厚勤俭，定为悠久人家。

【今文解译】　谨慎地恪守父亲与兄长的教诲，沉稳笃实，谦虚恭敬，就是性情温良为人敦厚的好子弟。
　　　　　　　不改变祖宗传下来的族规家法，守信厚道，勤俭节约，就一定能成为久享美誉的好人家。

【English Translation】

A boy that is called the young man of honesty and modesty must be the one who strictly adheres to what has been instructed by his father and elder brothers, and conducts himself in a way of being steadfast and modest.

A family that is called the household enjoying longtime reputation must be the one that holds fast to the rules and disciplines handed down from its ancestors, and runs the domestic affairs with honesty and frugality.

69. 莲朝开而暮合　草冬枯而春荣

69. Lotus flowers bloom in the morning and shut in the evening; grasses flourish in spring and wither in winter.

莲朝开而暮合，至不能合，则将落矣；富贵而无收敛意者，尚其鉴之。
草春荣而冬枯，至于极枯，则又生矣；困穷而有振兴志者，亦如是也。

【今文解译】　莲花早晨绽放傍晚闭合，等到不再闭合时，便就要凋谢了；有钱有地位却不懂得收敛的，正应以此为鉴，好好反省。
　　　　　　草木春天茂盛冬天枯败，等到完全枯败时，便就要重生了；身处穷困但不失振兴之志的，不妨学学草木这种精气神。

【English Translation】

Lotus flowers bloom in the morning and shut in the evening, and are to fade when they can no longer shut. The man of wealth and rank who does not know how to restrain himself had better take lotus flowers as a mirror for reflection. Grasses flourish in spring and wither in winter, and will rise again when they cannot wither any more. The man who is in a tight corner yet still aspires to brace up had better encourage himself with grasses and act as they do.

70. 自伐自矜当戒　我自求仁求义

70. Guard against the habit of boasting and cultivate yourself with benevolence and righteousness.

伐字从戈，矜字从矛，自伐自矜者，可为大戒；仁字从人，义（義）字从我，讲仁讲义者，不必远求。

【今文解译】　伐字的右边是"戈"，矜字的左边是"矛"；自伐与自矜都有自我炫耀的意思，沾上这种习气诚可谓大忌。

仁字的左边是"人"，义（義）字的下边是"我"；追求仁义的人不必好高骛远，能够从"我"做起就好。

【English Translation】

Pretentiousness and boastfulness are the two words full of untoward capacity. Those who have the habit to brag about themselves should keep a careful eye on them.

Benevolence and righteousness are the two words about the humans including "I". Those who cherish both do not have to go far away to seek them, just start where the "I" is.

71. 贫寒更须读书　富贵不忘稼穑

71. Study harder when poor and don't forget the hardship of farmwork when rich.

家纵贫寒，也须留读书种子①；人虽富贵，不可忘稼穑②艰辛。

【中文注释】　① 读书种子：此处喻要让孩子读书识字，接受文化教育。
　　　　　　　② 稼穑：耕种与收割。

【今文解译】　家里再穷也要让自己的子孙读书。
　　　　　　　人再富贵也不能忘了种地的艰辛。

【English Translation】

A family must let its sons and grandsons learn how to read and write no matter how poor it might be.

A man should never forget the hardships to labor in the field no matter how rich and powerful he might be.

72. 俭可养廉　静能生悟

72. Thrift helps to nourish the character of incorruptibility; quiet helps to breed the sense of the world.

俭可养廉,觉茅舍竹篱,自饶清趣；静能生悟,即鸟啼花落,都是化机。一生快活皆庸福,万种艰辛出伟人。

【今文解译】　俭朴可以培养一个人的廉洁品德,即使居住的是竹篱茅舍,也能感受到淡淡的乐趣。
守静常使人有所领悟,即使是鸟的啼鸣和花的凋落,也都能给人带来造化的生机。
一辈子快快乐乐是平凡人的福分,使一个人伟大的是他所经历的千辛万苦。

【English Translation】

Practicing thrift helps to nourish the character of incorruptibility. Even dwelling in a cottage fenced with bamboo, one can still feel about the plain amusement thereby.
Preserving the soul quiet helps to breed the sense of the world. Even in a spot where there is only twitter of birds and falling of flowers, one can still comprehend the vigor of Nature.
A lifelong happiness is the bliss a mortal would most like to have. What make a man great are the numerous hardships he has gone through.

73. 助人在于有心　虑事在于精详

73. Helping others is all about the heart; considering a thing is all about the accurateness and carefulness.

济世虽乏赀财，而存心方便，即称长者；生资虽少智慧，而虑事精详，即是能人。

【今文解译】　虽然没有济世救人的财力，但却存有乐于助人的心愿，这样的人堪称长者。
虽然生来就没什么天资，但考虑起问题来却周全细致，这样的人也即能人。

【English Translation】

You may be a person short of money and unable to donate people. But so long as you have the conscience to help them, you can still be held in esteem.
You may be a person wanting in wisdom and unable to offer good ideas. But so long as you have the habit to think carefully, you can still be called a talent.

74. 常怀振奋心　多说切直话

74. Always keep in mind your lofty aspirations and speak as earnestly as you can.

　　一室闲居，必常怀振卓心，才有生气；同人聚处，须多说切直话，方见古风。

【今文解译】　　即使只是独处一隅，也常常要有志存高远的胸怀，这样人才会显得生气勃勃。

与人相处时，要尽量多说些实实在在的话，这样才不失古代圣贤的大家风范。

【English Translation】

Staying alone at leisure, one must always keep in mind some lofty aspirations, thereby deserving to be addressed as a man full of vital energy.

Getting along with others, one must be earnest and fair-minded in conversations, thereby deserving to be taken as a model with ancient style.

75. 虚怀若谷即才德　骄奢淫逸枉富贵

75. It's a virtue to be modest and a shame to be arrogant when rich and powerful.

观周公①之不骄不吝②，有才何可自矜③？观颜子④之若无若虚⑤，为学岂容自足？门户之衰，总由于子孙之骄惰；风俗之坏，多起于富贵之奢淫。

【中文注释】　① 周公：也即周公旦，周武王的弟弟，为周朝之初政权的巩固做出了卓越的贡献。
② 不骄不吝：不骄横，不吝啬。
③ 自矜：自负。
④ 颜子：即颜回，孔子最得意的门生。
⑤ 若无若虚：意为"有才若无，有德若虚"，是对颜回谦虚品质的褒奖词。

【今文解译】　周公尚能不骄不吝，那些稍有才能的人凭什么自命不凡？
颜回尚且有才若无、有德若虚，那些为学的又怎能自满？
一个家庭的衰落往往是由于子孙后代的骄横懒惰。
社会风俗的败坏大多发端于富贵所致的奢华淫逸。

【English Translation】

Compared with Duke of Zhou* who, even with a great talent, never acted in a way of arrogance and stinginess, how can a slighted talented man pride himself on being out of the ordinary?

Compared with Yan Yuan who spent all his life in practicing modesty, how can a man devoting himself to academic pursuit be self-satisfied?

The decline of a family is always resulted from the young generations' haughtiness and indolence.

The corruption of social morals is often caused by the extravagance and dissipation of the rich and honorable.

【 English Annotation 】

* Duke of Zhou (fl. 1100BC), named Ji Dan, a sage of the Zhou Dynasty who played a major role in consolidating the kingdom established by his elder brother King Wu, also known as Duke Dan of Zhou or Zhou Gongdan.

76. 凝浩然正气　法古今完人

76. Cultivate yourself with uprightness and learn from the men of perfect morality.

孝子忠臣，是天地正气所钟①，鬼神亦为之呵护；圣经贤传②，乃古今命脉③所系，人物④悉赖以裁成。

【中文注释】　① 正气所钟：正气所聚之处。
　　　　　　② 圣经贤传：圣贤留下来的经典和著作。
　　　　　　③ 命脉：命根子；根本。
　　　　　　④ 人物：此处系指优秀人才或风流人物。

【今文解译】　孝子和忠臣都是天地间浩然正气之所在，连鬼神对他们都另眼相待，呵护有加。
　　　　　　圣贤的经典是自古及今一以贯之的命脉所系，历朝历代的风流人物无不受其熏染而得以扬名立万。

【English Translation】

Filial sons and loyal subjects are the two darlings raised by the righteousness of the heaven and earth. Even the ghosts and spirits baby them in every possible way.

Saints' classics are the lifeblood of society both in the past and at present. All the outstanding personages of the times pay homage to them and draw nutrition from them.

77. 饱暖则气昏志惰　饥寒则神紧骨坚

77. People tend to be indolent when well fed and will be firm-minded when hungry and cold.

饱暖人所共羡，然使享一生饱暖，而气昏志惰①，岂足有为？饥寒人所不甘，然必带几分饥寒，则神紧骨坚②，乃能任事③。

【中文注释】　①气昏志惰：无精打采，慵懒怠惰。
　　　　　　　②神紧骨坚：精神抖擞，体魄健壮。
　　　　　　　③乃能任事：方能委以重任；方能担当重任。

【今文解译】　人人都想过衣食无忧的生活，然而一辈子都衣食无忧却
　　　　　　　会使人意志消沉、精神颓废，怎么能有所作为？！
　　　　　　　谁都不想过饥寒交迫的日子，然而只有经历些饥寒之苦，
　　　　　　　人的精神才会振作起来，才有体魄担当重任。

【English Translation】

To have adequate food and clothing is a kind of life everyone admires. Nevertheless, what can one amount to if one only has a life as sufficient as such all his life but ever remains lackadaisical and unwilling to work?
Hunger and cold are what everyone hates. Nevertheless, one can only be entrusted with important things when one has experienced some sufferings of hunger and cold and proved oneself a man with lifted spirits and fine physique.

78. 愁烦中具潇洒襟怀　暗昧处见光明世界

78. Be easy and unrestrained when in a bad mood and open and above board when in a benighted circumstance.

　　愁烦中具潇洒襟怀，满抱皆春风和气；暗昧①处见光明世界，此心即白日青天。

【中文注释】　　① 暗昧：昏暗。此处用以形容处境的恶劣与黑暗。

【今文解译】　　忧愁烦闷的时候仍能保持潇洒豁达的气度，人就会有怀抱和煦春风的感觉。
　　　　　　　　在暗昧的处境中保持光明磊落的胸襟，人的内心就会像青天白日一般透亮。

【English Translation】

Be easy and unrestrained when in a melancholy mood, and you will feel as if you are hugging the spring breeze brimmed with warm and gentleness.
Be open and above board when in a benighted circumstance, and you will feel as if your heart is as bright as the daylight shining under the blue sky.

79. 势利人行为虚假　虚浮者一事无成

79. A snob behaves falsely while a pompous fellow can be nowhere.

势利人装腔做调，都只在体面上铺张，可知其百为皆假；虚浮人指东画西，全不向身心内打算，定卜其一事无成。

【今文解译】　势利的人做事总爱装腔作势，只会做表面文章。由此可知，这样的人做什么都是假惺惺的。

虚浮的人做事漫无头绪，心里完全没有计划和目标。据此可以料定，这样的人终将一事无成。

【English Translation】

The snobs love to put on frills and assume presentable looks, all appearing to be superficial and showy. Thus we know whatever they do is nothing but a sham.

The men fond of exaggeration tend to do things in a way of pointing to east and rushing to west and never have a set objective inwardly. Thus we predict they will accomplish nothing.

80. 不忮不求　勿忘勿助

80. Be neither jealous nor covetous of what others have; keep the heart quiet and let it be as it was.

不忮不求①，可想见光明境界；勿忘勿助②，是形容涵养功夫。

【中文注释】　① 不忮不求：意为既不嫉妒也不希求别人的财物。

② 勿忘勿助：是指在修炼之中，对于身体内的变化保持自然的口诀。张三丰曾说："神息相依，守其清静自然曰勿忘，顺其清静自然曰勿助。"

【今文解译】　对别人的财物不忮不求，可以看出一个人心灵世界的磊落。

能在个人的修炼中做到勿忘勿助，是涵养功夫到家的表现。

【English Translation】

Being neither jealous nor covetous of what others have is the indication of a bright and clean mind.

Keeping the heart quiet and allowing it to go as it will is the description of the height of moral cultivation.

81. 求其理则数难违　守其常变亦能御

81. Man's fate is predestined and irresistible; stick to the routine, and no unforeseen event cannot be dealt with.

　　数①虽有定，而君子但求其理②，理既得，数亦难违③；变④固宜防，而君子但守其常⑤，常无失，变亦能御。

【中文注释】　① 数：运数；命数。
　　　　　　　② 理：道理。此处可理解为运道中的因果关系。
　　　　　　　③ 难违：不可违背；不好或不会违背。
　　　　　　　④ 变：变故；变数。
　　　　　　　⑤ 常：常理；常规。

【今文解译】　人的运道是有定数的，但只要君子弄清楚运道中的因果关系并遵循行事，运道也就不会违背他的心愿。
　　　　　　　事物的变数固然应当预防，但只要君子能以守常的心态对待它并做到常道不失，变数也就不难应对了。

【English Translation】

Man's fate is predestined, but if a gentleman can sort out the cause and effect in the fate and do things by following the causal relationship, the fate will not defy him.

There should be a plan to guard against unforeseen event; but if a gentleman can act in accordance with the routine, then no unforeseen event cannot be dealt with.

82. 和气为祥　骄气为衰

82. Gentleness stands for the auspiciousness while arrogance, the decline.

　　和①为祥气，骄②为衰气，相人者③不难以一望而知；善是吉星，恶是凶星，推命者④岂必因五行⑤而定。

【中文注释】　① 和：和平；和睦；和气。
　　　　　　　② 骄：骄横；骄奢；骄傲。
　　　　　　　③ 相人者：看相算命的。
　　　　　　　④ 推命者：占卜的。
　　　　　　　⑤ 五行：金、木、水、火、土。中国古代哲学家用以说明世界万物的形成及其相互关系的理论。它强调整体概念，旨在描述事物的运动形式以及转化关系。

【今文解译】　和睦代表祥瑞之气，骄横代表衰败之气。看相的人只需一眼就能看出它们之间的区别。
　　　　　　　善良是吉星，邪恶是凶星。占卜的人即使不推演五行术也能确定哪是吉星，哪是凶星。

【English Translation】

Gentleness stands for the atmosphere of auspiciousness while arrogance, the atmosphere of decline. A fortune-teller can easily tell this from that even by one sight.
Kindness is leading to a good fortune while viciousness, to a bad fortune. A diviner can lightly divine which is which even without reasoning the Five Elements*.

【English Annotation】

* The Five Elements are referred to metal, wood, water, fire and earth. Ancient Chinese thinkers tried to use the concept or theory of these five substances to compose the physical universe and explain the origin of all things. Traditional

Chinese medical practitioners used the five elements to explain various physiological and pathological phenomena. Superstitious people used the principle of the five elements producing and overcoming each other to tell the fate of a person.

83. 人生不可安闲　日用必须简省

83. One should not rest content with a leisurely life but should be frugal in daily life.

　　人生不可安闲①，有恒业②，才足收放心；日用必须简省，杜奢端③，即以昭俭德。

【中文注释】　① 安闲：安于清闲。
　　　　　　② 恒业：可以维持生计的营生。
　　　　　　③ 杜奢端：远离奢侈。

【今文解译】　人生不可太安逸，而应有一份可供长久经营的事业，这样才能收住放逸的心。
　　　　　　日常用度要坚持简单节省，凡事切不可铺张浪费，这样才能彰显俭朴的美德。

【English Translation】

One should not rest content with the leisurely life he lives but should instead undertake a permanent enterprise; only in this way can one resume his drifting mind.

One should stay away with luxury by leading a simple life; only in this way can one make clear to all that he has the virtue of practicing thrift.

84. 卓有成就　铁面无私

84. To make a great achievement, one must be selfless and fearless.

　　成大事功，全仗着秤心斗胆；有真气节，才算得铁面铜头。

【今文解译】　　成大事凭的全是过人胆识。
　　　　　　　　有气节才称得上无私无畏。

【English Translation】

One who is determined to make a great achievement should do it with firm resolution and superior judgment.

Only when a man has obtained the quality of absolute uprightness can he become selfless and fearless.

85. 责己不责人则成　信己不信人则败

85. Blaming only oneself rather than others produces success; believing only in oneself rather than others results in failure.

但责己，不责人，此远怨之道也；但信己，不信人，此取败之由也。

【今文解译】　遇事就检讨自己，不责备别人，这是远离怨恨的做法。
　　　　　　做事只相信自己，不相信别人，这是招致失败的原因。

【English Translation】

Blaming only oneself rather than others is a good way to keep a grudge at a distance.
Believing only in oneself rather than others is the same as working one's own undoing.

86. 通达事理　无做作气

86. Be a man who is full of sense and unaffected.

无执滞^①心，才是通方士；有做作气，便非本色^②人。

【中文注释】　① 执滞：执拗；冥顽不化；一根筋。
　　　　　　　② 本色：本来面貌；没有虚假成分。

【今文解译】　不纠结于一得一失的人，才是通晓事理的人。
　　　　　　　动辄矫揉造作的人，肯定不是朴实无华的人。

【English Translation】

A sensible person is the one who has freed oneself from entanglement.
A sanctimonious person is the one who has the habit to overdo his acting.

87. 正直之心　留名后世

87. Be a man of integrity and make a good name for yourself after death.

　　耳目口鼻，皆无知识之辈，全靠着心作主人；身体发肤，总有毁坏之时，要留个名称后世。

【今文解译】　　耳目口鼻都是没有思想的，全靠心智做它们的主人。
　　　　　　　　身体发肤总有腐朽的一天，但要留个好名声在世上。

【English Translation】

The ears, eyes, mouth and nose are the sense organs without thought. They function only according to the will of the heart.

Since the hairs and skin are part of the flesh and will perish someday, one should make an untainted name for himself after death.

88. 后天需努力　小节要谨慎

88. Do work hard and be cautious about the trifles.

有生资，不加学力，气质究难化也；慎大德，不矜细行，形迹终可疑也。

【今文解译】　光有好的天资而不知道在学习上狠下功夫，人的气质终
究难以升华。
只注意大的德行而忽略小的行为举止，能否有得体的表
现值得怀疑。

【 English Translation 】

If a man born with gift can't devote himself to learning, his further quality
improvement will be impossible.
If a man only cares about great virtues but neglects minor points of conduct,
that he will behave well is doubtful.

89. 忠厚受人尊敬　平淡趣味深长

89. Loyalness is worth respecting while plainness has more taste.

　　世风之狡诈多端，到底忠厚人颠扑不破；末俗以繁华相尚，终觉冷淡处趣味弥长。

【今文解译】　尽管世人变得越来越狡诈，但为人忠厚的人还是能够坚守自己的做人准则不改初衷。

当今的人们极尽繁华奢侈之能事，但还是有人觉得清淡简朴的生活才更加意味深长。

【English Translation】

The world is becoming more and more deceptive, but still there are ones who are honest and loyal and stick to their normal practice.

Today's people do their best to be prosperous and luxurious, but still there is much food for thought so far as a plain life is concerned.

90. 交正直友　学德高人

90. Make friends with honest people and follow the men of high moral character.

能结交直道朋友，其人必有令名；肯亲近耆德老成，其家必多善事。

【今文解译】　能与品行端正的人交朋友，这样的人也一定有良好的口碑。
能与年高德劭的老者亲近，这样的人家一定有积善的美德。

【 English Translation 】

A man who can befriend the honest and upright is surely the one who has a good reputation.
A family that is close to highly respected old men is certainly the one that often performs good deeds.

91. 解邻里纷争　说因果关系

91. Disputes between neighbors should be settled through explanation of the rotation of karma.

为乡邻解纷争，使得和好如初，即化人①之事也；为世俗②谈因果，使知报应不爽③，亦劝善之方也。

【中文注释】　① 化人：化解人们心中的矛盾和疑虑。
　　　　　　　② 世俗：此处喻没有佛教信仰的人们。
　　　　　　　③ 不爽：没有失误；如期而至。

【今文解译】　为乡邻解决纠纷和争执，使他们和好如初，这也即尽到了化解矛盾的责任。
　　　　　　　向世人讲解因果报应的理念，使其明白报应不爽的道理，这也即劝人向善。

【English Translation】

It's a matter of dispelling misgivings to settle the disputes between fellow townsmen and make those who get involved in them reconciled as ever.

It's a way of exhorting people to do good to explain the rotation of karma to non-religious people and tell them how unfailing the retribution will be.

92. 发达需要努力　福寿也靠积德

92. Development and flourishing need efforts; fortune and longevity depend on virtue.

发达虽命定，亦由肯做功夫；福寿虽天生，还是多积阴德。

【今文解译】　人的飞黄腾达虽然是命中注定的, 但也离不开个人的发
　　　　　　　奋努力。
　　　　　　　人的福祉和寿数虽然是上天安排的, 但还是要坚持多行
　　　　　　　善积德。

【English Translation】

Personal prosperity is decided by destiny; but still one cannot succeed in obtaining it if without painstaking efforts.

Man's fortune and lifespan are a matter of fate; but still one should do as many good deeds as possible to back it up.

93. 百善孝为先　万恶淫为首

93. Filial piety is the most important of all virtues; Lewdness is the worst of all sins.

常存仁孝心，则天下凡不可为者皆不忍为，所以孝居百行之先；一起邪淫念，则生平极不欲为者皆不难为，所以淫是万恶之首。

【今文解译】　心中常存仁孝之心，凡世界上不该做的事情就都不会去做，所以才有"百善孝为先"这一说。

心中一旦起了淫念，平时极不愿意去做的事情也都会去做，所以才有"万恶淫为源"这一说。

【English Translation】

Keep filial piety in mind constantly, and one will not bear to do what is prohibited across the world. That's why people say filial piety is the most essential of all virtues.

Once lewdness steals into the heart, one would feel no difficult to do what one hates to do at ordinary times. So goes the saying that lewdness is the worst of all sins.

94. 自奉减几分　处世退一步

94. In getting along with others, it's better to conduct yourself in a concessive way.

自奉必减几分方好，处世能退一步为高。

【今文解译】　　自己的花销能减去就减去些, 这才见好。
为人处世能退一步就退一步, 不失高明。

【English Translation】

In working out a budget of living for oneself, it's quite proper to lower some standards.
In getting along with others, it's quite smart to conduct yourself in a concessive way.

95. 持守本分安贫乐道　凡事忍让长久不衰

95. Know your poverty and remain happy; forbear for long-term prosperity.

　　安分守贫，何等清闲，而好事者偏自寻烦恼；持盈保泰，总须忍让，而恃强者乃自取灭亡。

【今文解译】　安守本分地乐对贫穷是何等清闲安逸，而好事之徒却偏偏要自寻烦恼。

事业极盛时想保持太平就少不得忍让，恃强逞能到头来只能自取灭亡。

【 English Translation 】

What a leisurely life it is to know one's place and remain happy in poverty! But unfortunately, there are some people who just like to make trouble to harass themselves.

When your enterprise reaches an extreme you must maintain your position by exercising forbearance. If you flaunt your superiority you are simply cutting your own throat.

96. 境遇无常　光阴易逝

96. Man's lot is changeable and fleet, man's life.

人生境遇无常，须自谋一吃饭本领；人生光阴易逝，要早定一成器日期。

【今文解译】　人生的境遇是变化无常的，所以必须学会一项能独自谋生的技能。

人的一生是很短暂的，所以应该对何时能实现个人价值早做谋划。

【English Translation】

Man's lot is so changeable that one ought to master a working skill to support oneself.

Man's life is so fleet that one should set a date for individual development as early as possible.

97. 川学海而至海　莠似苗而非苗

97. All the rivers follow the sea's example and run into it; bristle grasses seem to be but are not seedlings of cereal crops.

川学海而至海，故谋道者不可有止心；莠非苗而似苗，故穷理者不可无真见。

【今文解译】 河川学习海洋的博大而流向海洋，所以，追求道之真义的人要有恒心，不可半途而废。
野草不是禾苗但却长得酷似禾苗，所以，探究事理的人要有辨别力，不可没有真知灼见。

【English Translation】

All the rivers follow the sea's example and run into it. So, in exploring the essence of the Way, we should not give up our effort halfway.
Bristle grasses seem to be but are not seedlings of cereal crops. So, in pursuing truth, we shouldn't be without real knowledge and deep insight.

98. 守身必谨严　养心须淡泊

98. Man's integrity must be maintained with great care while cultivation of the mind needs no fame and fortune.

守身必谨严，凡足以戕吾身者宜戒之；养心须淡泊，凡足以累吾心者勿为也。

【今文解译】　保持节操必须谨慎严密；凡是有损自己节操的行为，都要予以戒除。
养心必须注重宁静淡泊；凡是有碍心性修炼的事，坚决不要去染指。

【English Translation】

Carefulness and preciseness are the two critical points in preserving moral integrity. Anything that might hinder our moral integrity should be guarded against.

Not wooing fame and fortune is what we must stick to in nourishing the heart. Anything that might impede our practice to nourish heart should be disregarded.

99. 有德不在有位　能行不在能言

99. It's important to have noble virtues rather than noble ranks and the ability to act rather than the ability to speak.

人之足传，在有德，不在有位；世所相信，在能行，不在能言。

【今文解译】　　一个人之所以值得称道，在于他的品德有多优秀，而不在于他的位分有多高。

一个人之所以得到世人的信任，在于他有怎样的行动，而不在于他如何能说。

【English Translation】

The reason why one deserves to be applauded is not that one has a noble rank but that one has noble virtues.

The one in whom people have belief is not he who is good at talking but he who is capable of acting.

100. 称誉易 无怨难

100. It is easy to win praise but hard to avoid resentment.

与其使乡党①有誉言②，不如令乡党无怨言；与其为子孙谋产业③，不如教子孙习恒业。

【中文注释】 ① 乡党: 本意为乡里乡亲。
② 誉言: 称誉的言辞。
③ 产业: 财产, 尤指不动产。

【今文解译】 与其刻意博取左邻右舍对你的赞许, 不如使他们对你的言行没有怨言。
与其为子孙后代积聚财富, 不如教育他们学习和掌握赖以谋生的技能。

【English Translation】

To be praised by the locals is not as good as to let them bear no grudge against us.
To accumulate wealth for our offspring is not as good as to instruct them to learn the skills to earn a living.

101. 多记先贤格言　闲看他人行事

101. Keep in heart the teachings of ancient sages and observe the ways of others to act.

多记先贤格言，胸中方有主宰；闲看他人行事，眼前即是规箴①。

【中文注释】　① 规箴：规，画图的器具；箴，具有规劝性质的文体。规箴是指行为准则。

【今文解译】　脑子里记下的先辈圣贤的教诲多了，心中自然就有主心骨了。
从旁观察别人的处事方式，自己的行为准则自然也就形成了。

【English Translation】

Only when one keeps in heart plenty of the teachings of ancient sages can one have a master for one's own mind.
One can form one's own principles for personal behavior by observing the ways and manners others act.

102. 身为重臣而精勤　面临大敌犹弈棋

102. An important official in the land should know how to keep calm in the face of a strong enemy.

陶侃①运甓②官斋，其精勤③可企而及④也；谢安⑤围棋别墅，其镇定非学而能⑥也。

【中文注释】

① 陶侃（259年—334年）：晋朝名将，为人明断果决，任广州刺史时，经常运砖修习精勤。

② 甓：砖的一种。

③ 精勤：专心勤勉。

④ 可企而及：能够做到；不难企及。

⑤ 谢安（320年—385年）：东晋著名政治家，淝水之役前夕，前秦苻坚投鞭断流，人心为之惶惶，当时身为征讨大都督的谢安，丝毫不惊慌，闲时仍与友人在别墅下棋，镇定如常，最后他的侄儿谢玄大破苻坚于淝水。

⑥ 非学而能：没有学习就会的（也即与生俱来的能耐）；无须学习就能掌握的。

【今文解译】 晋朝名将陶侃任广州刺史时，为了磨炼自己的意志，每天清晨亲手将一堆砖头从室内搬至室外，傍晚再把它们搬回室内。他的这种精勤我们是可以做到的。而东晋著名政治家谢安在大敌当前时，仍能和人在他的别墅里下棋对弈。他的这种临危不乱的镇定却不是通过一般的学习就能做到的。

【English Translation】

The diligence with which Tao Kan*, merely to steel himself, moved everyday a pile of bricks from his study to the courtyard in the morning and moved them back in the evening is what we can imitate. While the easy-possessed mien with which Xie An* played chess with his friend in his villa the very moment a large enemy force was bearing down upon the border is what we can not take after.

112

【 English Annotation 】

* Tao Kan (259-334), a famous general of the Eastern Jin Dynasty, well known for his courageousness and resoluteness in military actions.
* Xie An (320-385), a famous statesman of the Eastern Jin Dynasty, and chief commander of Jin's army in the Battle of Fei River in 383, where Fu Jian and his troops of the Former Qin was defeated by the numerically inferior Jin's army.

103. 有济人之心　无欺人之意

103. One should have the heart to donate others rather than the intention to bully them.

　　但患我不肯济人，休患我不能济人；须使人不忍欺我，勿使人不敢欺我。

【今文解译】　要担心自己不肯帮人，而不要担心自己帮不了人。
　　　　　　　要使别人不忍心欺辱我，而不要使人不敢欺辱我。

【English Translation】

What worries me is not that I am unable to help others, but that I refuse to help when I am able to.
What values is not that I make others not dare to humiliate me, but that I make them not bear to do so.

104. 能读书即有福　教子弟即创家

104. To read and learn is to invite happiness; to educate kids is to build the family.

何谓享福之人，能读书者便是；何谓创家之人，能教子者便是。

【今文解译】　什么样的人是有福可享的人？能够读书学习的人是有福可享的人。

什么样的人是创立家业的人？能够管教子女的人是创立家业的人。

【English Translation】

Who is he that is called the man able to enjoy happiness? The one that can read and learn is.

Who is he that is called the builder of a family? The one that knows how to educate his kids is.

105. 教子勿溺爱　子堕莫弃绝

105. Don't spoil your children and give them up when they degenerate.

　　子弟①天性未漓，教易入也，则体孔子之言以劳之②（爱之，能勿劳乎③？），勿溺爱以长其自肆④之心。子弟习气已坏，教难行也，则守孟子之言以养之⑤（中也养不中，才也养不才⑥），勿轻弃以绝其自新之路。

【中文注释】　　① 子弟：对父兄而言，即子与弟. 泛指年轻后辈。

　　② 劳之：此处喻严格管教之。

　　③ 爱之能勿劳乎：出自孔子第 10 世孙孔安国的《论语孔氏训解》，意即（我）爱他，我能不（为他）操劳吗?！

　　④ 自肆：自我放纵；缺乏自我约束力。

　　⑤ 养之：感化之。

　　⑥ 中也养不中，才也养不才：出自《孟子·离娄章句下》。意即品德修养好的人教育熏陶品德修养不好的人；有才能的人教育熏陶没有才能的人。

【今文解译】　　当年轻后辈的天性尚未被浸染时就开始对他们的教育，这并不难。此时家长要做的就是按照孔子所说的"爱之，能勿劳乎"去教导他们，切不可因为溺爱而使他们滋长自我放纵的习气。等到他们沾染上不良习气才开始教育他们，那就难了。这种情况下，家长要做的就是按照孟子所说的"中也养不中，才也养不才"去开导他们，决不可轻易放弃而使他们失去自新的机会。

【English Translation】

It's not difficult to start the education of a child when his inborn nature remains unstained. Under this circumstance, what the patriarch should do is to train him strictly in accordance with the principles Confucius proposed (referring to his words as of "If l love him, how can I not take care of him?") and never abet his willfulness out of undue love.

It's difficult to conduct the education of a child when he has contracted a bad habit. If this be the case, what the patriarch should do is to affect him with good examples in the way Mencius suggested (referring to his words as of "Men of lofty morality should educate and influence men of doubtful morality and men of talent should educate and influence untalented men.") and never let go off any chance to lead him to the road of a new life.

106. 专心可立功　偏见易败事

106. Concentration is the road to success; prejudice is a slippery slope.

忠实而无才①，尚可立功，心志专一②也；忠实而无识③，必至偾事④，意见多偏也。

【中文注释】　① 无才: 没有能力。
　　　　　　　② 心志专一: 专心致志; 一心一意; 心无旁骛。
　　　　　　　③ 无识: 缺乏见识; 没有主意; 头脑简单。
　　　　　　　④ 偾事: 败事; 把事情搞糟。

【今文解译】　忠实可靠但却没有才能的人还是可以建立功业的, 这是因为他们的心志是专一的。
　　　　　　　忠实可靠但却没有见识的人必然不足以成事, 这是因为他们的想法往往是偏废的。

【English Translation】

He that is faithful and honest but not capable enough may as well accomplish some things so long as he fully devotes himself to what he is doing.
He that is faithful and honest yet wanting in sense will surely have prejudices against the things he is doing and thus mess them up in the end.

107. 不忘艰难之境　不存侥幸之心

107. Don't forget the existence of adversity and take chances in doing things.

　　人虽无艰难之时，却不可忘艰难之境；世虽有侥幸之事，断不可存侥幸之心。

【今文解译】　尽管自己从未遇到过什么艰难困苦，但还是不能忘记艰难困苦是确实存在的。
　　　　　　　世界上确实有因侥幸而功成名就的事，但做事光凭侥幸心理却是万万不可的。

【English Translation】

One should never forget the existence of adversity even if staying in a circumstance free of adversity.
One should never be dependent on luck even if there are indeed some things that came off by luck.

108. 心静则明　品超斯远

108. Man's heart will be clear the minute it calms down; a noble character can rise above the material desires.

心静则明，水止乃能照物；品超斯远^①，云飞而不碍空。

【中文注释】　① 品超斯远：高尚的品格可以克服物欲的影响。

【今文解译】　心平静了就自然会亮堂，如同池水静止了就能够鉴照万物。

品格高尚了就会超脱，就像云彩飞来飞去但从不堵塞天空。

【English Translation】

Man's heart will be clear the minute it calms down. It's just the same as the water which can mirror objects clearly when it is in stillness.

A high-level moral standing can transcend the material desires. It's like the free flying of the clouds which by no means obstruct the sky.

109. 贫乃顺境　俭即丰年

109. Poverty is good for reading; frugality is equivalent to abundance.

清贫乃读书人顺境，节俭即种田人丰年①。

【中文注释】　①丰年：米谷收成丰盛的年景。

【今文解译】　对读书人来说，清贫就是大好时光。

对种田人来说，节俭也即五谷丰登。

【English Translation】

Impoverished circumstance is the condition favorable for the man of culture to devote himself to his study.

Practicing thrift is the means by which the farmer is enabled to reap another harvest out of the same year.

110. 常有正直心　莫有浮华志

110. Be honest and down-to-earth but don't be hollow and superficial.

正而过则迂，直而过则拙，故迂拙之人，犹不失为正直。高或入于虚，华或入于浮，而虚浮之士，究难指为高华。

【今文解译】　做人过于刚正就会显得迂腐，过于直率就会显得笨拙。所以，迂腐和笨拙的人，其本质上还是刚正直率的。

高深很可能会蜕变成虚空，华丽很可能会蜕变成浮浅。

然而，虚夸和浮浅终究不能够被看作是高深和华丽。

【English Translation】

Excessive straightforwardness often looks like pedantry, and over-uprightness often looks like clumsiness. Nevertheless, the men of pedantry and those of clumsiness are the two kinds who can still be considered as straightforward and upright.

Profoundness is very likely to degenerate into hollowness, and gorgeousness is very likely to degenerate into superficiality. Nevertheless, hollowness and superficiality can never be regarded as profound and gorgeous after all.

111. 异端背乎经常　邪说涉于虚诞

111. Things against the set norms and conventions are called heterodoxy and those relating to fabrication and preposterousness are called heresy.

人知佛老①为异端②，不知凡背乎经常者，皆异端也；人知杨墨③为邪说④，不知凡涉于虚诞者，皆邪说也。

【中文注释】　① 佛老: 系指佛教和道教以及它们各自的学说。
② 异端: 本意是指不符合正统思想的主张或教义。古代儒家习惯称其他学说、学派为异端。
③ 杨墨: 系指杨朱与墨翟两位战国时的哲学家和思想家，诸子百家中的佼佼者。（杨墨二人的学说与孔子的儒家思想在许多方面是格格不入的, 故身为儒家学子的作者将其贬为邪说。——译注）
④ 邪说: 泛指存乎于正统学说之外的学说。

【今文解译】　人们都知道佛教和老子学说是异端, 但不知道凡是离经叛道的, 其实都属于异端。
人们都知道杨朱和墨翟的思想是邪说, 但不知道凡是虚妄荒诞的, 其实都是邪说。

【English Translation】

People only know that the doctrines of Buddhism and Taoism* are heterodox, but do not know that things against the set norms and conventions are also called heterodoxy.
People only know that the theories of Yang Zhu* and Mo Zi* are fallacies, but do not know that things relating to fabrication and preposterousness are also called heresy.

【English Annotation】

* Taoism, or Daoism, is a philosophical, ethical, and religious tradition of

Chinese origin that emphasizes living in harmony with the Tao (also romanized as Dao).

* Yang Zhu (?-?), a philosopher in the Warring States Period, whose views and opinions against Confucianism and Moism were sparsely seen in the classical works such as *Lie Zi, Mencius, Zhuang Zi, Hanfeizi* and *The Spring and Autumn of Lü Buwei*, also known as Yang Zi.

* Mo Zi (c. 468BC-c. 376BC), named Mo Di, a thinker, educator, scientist, military strategist and statesman during the Warring States Period, and founder of Moism, also known as Mozi or Mocius.

112. 亡羊尚可补牢 羡鱼何如结网

112. It's never too late to mend the fold even after the sheep is lost; to stand by a river to dream of fish is not as good as going home to knit fishnet.

图功①未晚，亡羊尚可补牢；浮慕②无成，羡鱼何如结网。

【中文注释】　①图功: 立志成就一番事业。
②浮慕: 只仰慕不实干; 空想。

【今文解译】　亡羊补牢尚且不晚，想干一番事业又有什么迟不迟的!
站在河边羡鱼不如回家编织渔网，空想只能一事无成。

【English Translation】

It's never too late to aspire for personal achievement, for one could mend the fold even after the sheep is lost.
Admiration alone is useless, for standing by a river to dream of fish is not as good as going home to knit fishnet.

113. 道本足于身　境难足于心

113. Substance in human nature is resourceful for moral cultivation; material affluence can hardly satisfy man's heart.

　　道本足于身，切实求来，则常若不足矣；境难足于心，尽行放下，则未有不足矣。

【今文解译】　人性中的道能够满足修身的需要,但若不断认真地求索,最终也还是会常常感到不足为用。
　　　　　　　物质条件再优裕也难满足人的欲望,但若能把所有的欲望都放下,人也就不再会贪心不足。

【English Translation】

The substance in human nature is resourceful for moral cultivation. But if one explores it in a down-to-earth way, he will often find it inadequate.
Material affluence can hardly satisfy man's heart. But if all the existing temptations are excluded man's heart will not be of avarice anymore.

114. 下苦功读书 有益于社会

114. To benefit the world, one must study hard.

　　读书不下苦功，妄想显荣，岂有此理？为人全无好处，欲邀福庆，从何得来？

【今文解译】　　一心想显达荣耀，但读书却又不肯下苦功夫，哪有这样的好事？！
从不做有益于别人的事，但却想得到别人的祝福，这怎么可能？！

【English Translation】

One hopes to achieve honor and glory but hates to make painstaking efforts in his study. Who ever heard of such a thing!
One wishes to have others' blessings but is unwilling to do anything good to them. How can this be possible?

115. 知错即改　不甘堕落

115. Correct the mistake when you know it and never abandon yourself to vice.

才觉己有不是，便决意改图，此立志为君子也；明知人议其非，偏肆行无忌，此甘心为小人也。

【今文解译】　　一发现自己有什么地方做得不对，就马上下决心改正，这是立志做个君子的表现。

明明知道有人在议论自己的不是，但却偏偏不知悔改，这是小人自甘堕落的做法。

【English Translation】

Making his mind to correct his own mistakes the moment being aware of them — this is the way how a true man becomes worthy of his name.
Knowing clearly the public censure on him but still persisting in his wrong doings — this is the way how a petty man remains to be of low origin.

116. 淡中交耐久　静里寿延长

116. Plain fellowship will ever last; life in peace will be prolonged.

淡中交耐久，静里寿延长。

【今文解译】　平淡中结下的友谊经得起时间的考验。
平静中与世无争的生活可以延年益寿。

【English Translation】

The fellowship will be ever so enduring if one can associate with others in a plain way.
The lifespan of a man will be ever so prolonged if one can lead a life in peace and ease.

117. 深思熟虑 以绝后患

117. To prevent future trouble, one must think carefully before acting.

　　凡遇事物突来，必熟思审处，恐贻后悔；不幸家庭衅起，须忍让曲全，勿失旧欢。

【今文解译】　遇到突如其来的事情，一定要深思熟虑后再采取谨慎的应对措施，不然恐遗憾将来。
　　　　　　　家庭内部发生纠葛，一定要顾全大局，忍让以对，切不可因此而失去了往日的和睦。

【English Translation】

When coming across some unexpected happenings, one should probe into it carefully before taking any actions, so as not to entail repentance onto the future.

When there unfortunately appears a dispute between family members, one should remove it by exercising forbearance, so as not to let it impair the domestic relations.

118. 聪明不外露　耕读可兼营

118. Farm work and academic study can run side by side.

聪明勿使外散，古人有纩以塞耳，旒以蔽目者矣；耕读何妨兼营，古人有出而负耒，入而横经①者矣。

【中文注释】　① 横经：本意为横陈经籍，此处泛指受业或读书。

【今文解译】　为了在人前不显得那么耳聪目明，自古就有人用丝棉球塞住自己的耳朵，用帽子的饰带遮掩自己的眼睛。

为了使种地和读书可以做到两不误，自古就有人白天扛着农具到地里去干活，晚上回到家中就挑灯苦读。

【 English Translation 】

Do not show off your talent if any. Just remember some people in ancient times, for the purpose of containing their talent, often used cotton fibers to stuff up their ears and tassels to shelter their eyes. Farm work and academic study can run side by side. The fact has it that some people in ancient times usually went to work in the field by day and bent their minds to their academic explorations by night.

119. 享受适可而止　学问永不知足

119. One should know how far to go in seeking enjoyment and never be satisfied in learning.

身不饥寒，天未尝负我；学无长进，我何以对天。

【今文解译】　身体无饥寒之忧, 那是老天没有待亏我; 如果学问无长进, 我该如何面对老天爷?!

【English Translation】

Free from hunger and cold, I'm in debt to the heaven. If I fail to make progress in my study, how can I face the heaven?

120. 勿与人争　惟求己知

120. Avoid competing with others about gains and losses only to increase your knowledge and ability.

　　不与人争得失，惟求己有知能。

【今文解译】　　不要为了个人的得失而去和别人争，而应该把心思都用在增加自己的智慧和才能上。

【English Translation】

Never intend to vie with others for personal gain and loss. Just bend your thoughts on how to increase your knowledge and ability.

121. 既中规中矩　又灵活变化

121. In social dealings, one should be both disciplined and flexible.

为人循矩度^①，而不见精神^②，则登场之傀儡也；做事守章程^③，而不知权变^④，则依样之葫芦也。

【中文注释】　① 循矩度：矩度，规矩法度；循矩度，循规蹈矩。
　　　　　　② 精神：精神所在；意义所在。
　　　　　　③ 章程：办事的规则。
　　　　　　④ 权变：通权达变。

【今文解译】　为人只知道循规蹈矩，而不知道规矩的要义所在，这样的人就只是舞台上的木偶而已。
　　　　　　做事一板一眼，而全然不知随机应变，这就像依葫芦画瓢一样，只是简单的模仿而已。

【English Translation】

Those who only conform to the set norms and conventions but see not the substance behind them are but the puppets on stage.

Those who stick to the old ways and refuse to make changes accordingly are simply imitating what was done by others.

122. 山水是文章化境　烟云乃富贵幻形

122. The mountains and waters are the magic subjects in literature.

山水是文章化境，烟云乃富贵幻形。

【今文解译】　一如山水是文人笔下的奇妙景色，烟云是富贵投在地上
　　　　　　　的幻影。

【English Translation】

As the mountains and waters are the magic subjects in literary writings, so the mist and clouds are the projection of wealth and rank.

123. 察人伦留心细微　化乡风道义为本

123. To observe the world interpersonally is to find out its small problems; to cultivate the countryside is to promote its moral education.

郭林宗①为人伦之鉴②，多在细微处留心；王彦方③化乡里之风④，是从德义中立脚。

【中文注释】　① 郭林宗：东汉介休人，范滂谓其"隐不违亲，贞不绝俗；天子不得臣，诸侯不得友"。生平好品题人物，而不为危言骇论，故党锢之祸得以独免。
② 人伦之鉴：处理人际关系的典范。
③ 王彦方：东汉太原人，名烈，平居以德行感化乡里，凡有争讼者，多趋而请教之，以判曲直。
④ 乡里之风：乡里之间的风气。

【今文解译】　郭林宗之所以被奉为处理人际关系的典范，就因为他能常常留心事情的细枝末节。
王彦方之所以能教化乡里的风气，靠的就是他能以道德和正义作为处世的立脚点。

【English Translation】

Guo Linzong* is the model in interpersonal relations. What he cared about is the minor issues others might neglect.
Wang Yanfang* plays a leading role in moral improving among his natives. What he relied on is morality and justice.

【English Annotation】

* Guo Linzong (128-169), a celebrity of the Eastern Han Dynasty, well versed in speech and personnel comment.
* Wang Yanfang (141-218), given name Lie, a native of the Eastern Han Dynasty, well devoted to promoting the development of good tendencies in his native land.

124. 勿妄行欺诈　不独享安闲

124. Don't cheat others and enjoy leisure alone.

天下无憨人，岂可妄行欺诈？世上皆苦人，何能独享安闲？

【今文解译】　谁都不是傻瓜，怎么能恣意妄为、蒙骗天下呢？！
世人谋生都很辛苦，怎么能一个人独享安闲呢？！

【English Translation】

There is no one in the world that is foolish. How can a fellow willfully deceive others by fair means or foul?

It is hard for the world to make a living. How can a guy enjoy alone a leisurely life without any compassion?

125. 忍让非懦弱　自大终糊涂

125. He who practices forbearance is never a coward; he who thinks himself important is after all a blunderer.

甘受人欺，定非懦弱；自谓予智，终是糊涂。

【今文解译】　　甘愿遭受欺侮的人，定非怯懦之辈。
　　　　　　　　自以为聪明的人，终究是个糊涂蛋。

【English Translation】

He who is willing to be blustered is never a coward.
He who thinks himself clever is after all a blunderer.

126. 功德文章　传诸后世

126. What can be passed on to later generations is only a man's deeds and words.

　　漫夸富贵显荣，功德文章要可传诸后世；任教声名煊赫，人品心术不能瞒过史官[①]。

【中文注释】　　① 史官：中国历代朝廷专门记录和编撰历史的官员。

【今文解译】　　富贵荣华不值一提，能流传给后世的是一个人的功德和文章。
　　　　　　　　一个人的声名即使再怎么显赫，他的人品心术也是瞒不过史官的。

【English Translation】

Wealth and splendor are not worth mentioning. What can be passed on to later generations is only a man's deeds and words.

No matter how popularized and celebrated a man might be, his inner power and true motives can not cheat historians.

127. 闭目养心　口阖防祸

127. Close your eyes to nourish the heart; close your mouth to prevent disasters.

神传于目，而目则有胞，闭之可以养神也；祸出于口，而口则有唇，阖之可以防祸也。

【今文解译】　人的神情靠眼睛来传递，而眼睛外面由上下两层眼睑护着，闭目则可以养神。
祸从口出，而嘴巴上下各有一片唇瓣，把嘴巴闭起来了则可以防止口舌之祸。

【English Translation】

Man's spirit is conveyed by the eyes which have eyelids without. Close the eyelids and one will attain mental tranquility.
Man's mouth, which has two lips without, is the source of trouble. Close the lips and one will be far away from the trouble.

128. 富贵难教子　贫穷要读书

128. It's difficult for rich people to bring up their children properly; poor scholars should be devoted to their academic pursuit.

富家惯习骄奢，最难教子；寒士欲谋生活，还是读书。

【今文解译】　富贵人家惯于奢侈豪华，因而也最难把自己的子孙教育好。

贫穷的读书人要想在社会上谋得一条生路，靠的还是读书。

【English Translation】

Rich people are used to wallowing in luxury and pleasure, so it's most difficult for them to bring up their children properly.

Poor scholars ought to be fully devoted to their academic pursuit if they want to earn a living as desired.

129. 苟且不能振　庸俗不可医

129. People who don't do their business can't cheer up; people of low taste can never be redeemed.

人犯一苟字，便不能振；人犯一俗字，便不可医。

【今文解译】　人一旦有了苟活的想法，便不再能振作起来。
人一旦沾染上低级趣味，便永远不可救药了。

【English Translation】

One can never bestir oneself unless one stops idling away time.
One can never be redeemed unless one dispenses the vulgar interests.

130. 有雄才者　必有大志

130. A man of great talent must have great ambition.

有不可及之志，必有不可及之功；有不忍言之心，必有不忍言之祸。

【今文解译】　有不可企及的志向，就一定有众所不及的雄才。
　　　　　　　有不忍道破的心结，就一定有恐遭祸患的隐衷。

【English Translation】

Whoever cherishes aspirations far beyond others' reach must have the ability to accomplish exploits unparalleled.

Whoever is reluctant to speak out what's on the inside must have a hidden fear of disaster which can not be disclosed.

131. 让退一步　容易处事

131. When a thing becomes difficult to deal with, a step back can make it easy.

事当难处之时，只让退一步，便容易处矣；功到将成之候，若放松一着，便不能成矣。

【今文解译】　事情棘手的时候，只需退让一步便可海阔天空。
　　　　　　　事业即将成功的时候，稍有松懈便会前功尽弃。

【English Translation】

When a thing becomes difficult to deal with, a step back can make it not difficult anymore.

When you are on the verge of success, even a minor laxation will bring all your previous efforts to naught.

132. 无学为贫　无德为孤

132. Poverty is the lack of knowledge; loneliness is that of virtue.

　　无财非贫，无学乃为贫；无位非贱，无耻乃为贱；无年非夭，无述乃为夭；无子非孤，无德乃为孤。

【今文解译】　没有财富不等于贫穷，不学无术才是真正的贫穷。

没有地位不等于低贱，不知廉耻才是真正的低贱。

寿数不长不等于短命，没有建树才是真正的短命。

没有子嗣不等于孤独，没有德性才是真正的孤独。

【English Translation】

One is poor not because of his pennilessness but because of his knowledgelessness.

One is lowly not because of his ranklessness but because of his shamelessness.

One is short-lived not because of his fortunelessness but because of his meritlessness.

One is lonely not because of his childlessness but because of his virtuelessness.

133. 知过能改　抑恶扬善

133. Correct the mistake when you know it and you can shun evil and promote good.

知过能改，便是圣人之徒①；恶恶②太严③，终为君子之病④。

【中文注释】　① 徒：追随者；信奉者；弟子。
② 恶恶：前"恶"作动词解，指厌恶；后"恶"作名词解，指恶人恶事。
③ 严：激烈。
④ 病：受害于。

【今文解译】　知道自己有错就改的人，就是圣人的信徒。
嫉恶如果太过严厉，终将成为君子的隐患。

【English Translation】

Correct the mistake when you know it and you will be a good follower of the sage.

Reproaching the vicious too severely will eventually become a hidden danger for a gentleman.

134. 诗书立业　孝悌做人

134. Classics are the basis of a man of knowledge and filial piety the pedestal of a man of virtue.

士必以诗书^①为性命^②，人须从孝悌立根基。

【中文注释】　① 诗书: 指《诗经》和《尚书》。此处泛指一切（儒家的）经书。
② 性命: 此处喻求知和治学的根本。

【今文解译】　要想成为饱学之士，就必须以诗书作为治学根本。
要想成为尚德之人，就必须从孝顺友爱开始做起。

【English Translation】

To be a man of culture, one must take all classics as the basis of his academic pursuit.
To be a man of virtue, one must take filial piety as the pedestal of his personality.

135. 得意勿忘形　苦心终有报

135. Don't get dizzy with success; you will be rewarded if you have done your best and most.

德泽^①太薄，家有好事，未必是好事，得意者何可自矜^②？天道最公，人能苦心^③，断不负苦心，为善者须当自信。

【中文注释】　① 德泽: 行善积德, 泽被他人。
　　　　　　② 自矜: 自以为了不起。
　　　　　　③ 苦心: 此处喻尽心尽力。

【今文解译】　德泽太薄的人家, 即使有好事降临也未必就是好事, 那些得意于一时一事的人有什么可值得夸耀的?!
　　　　　　上天是最讲公道的, 如果人能恪尽职守, 上天就一定不会辜负于他, 与人为善的人对此应当充满自信。

【English Translation】

It is not necessarily a good thing for a family of few kindness and charity to have a good thing. How can those who are easily turned by a small achievement think themselves terrific?

The way of heaven is fairest and never fails to reward the ones who have done their best and most. Therefore, those who are doing good deeds should have confidence in themselves.

136. 自知之明　不卑不亢

136. People should know themselves well and be neither haughty nor humble.

把自己太看高了，便不能长进；把自己太看低了，便不能振兴①。

【中文注释】　①振兴：振作起来。

【今文解译】　把自己看得过高, 则今后难有长进; 把自己看得过低, 则会失去振作的动力。

【English Translation】

One can hardly make any progress if one overestimates oneself. Likewise, one can never rouse to action if one underestimates oneself.

137. 有为之士不轻为　好事之人非晓事

137. A promising person is one who never act recklessly while a troublemaker one who has no common sense.

古今有为之士，皆不轻为之士；乡党好事之人，必非晓事之人。

【今文解译】　古往今来的有为之士, 都不是轻举妄动的人。
同乡同里的好事之徒, 定是些不明事理的人。

【English Translation】

Ever since ancient times, the promising characters have been only referred to the ones who never act recklessly.
In a village or a town, those who are meddlesome must be the ones who cannot weigh the ins and outs.

138. 勿因噎废食　莫讳疾忌医

138. We should not give up eating for fear of choking and refuse to accept treatment for fear that others will know about our illness.

偶缘^①为善受累^②，遂无意为善，是因噎废食也；明识有过当规，却讳言有过，是讳疾忌医^③也。

【中文注释】　① 偶缘：偶尔因为。
　　　　　　② 为善受累：做了好事反被误解。
　　　　　　③ 讳疾忌医：生怕别人知道自己的病情而拒绝就医。

【今文解译】　偶尔因为做善事而遭受委屈，便不愿意继续做好事，这是典型的因噎废食。
　　　　　　明明知道有过错就应该纠正，却绝口不提自己有错，这是纯粹的讳疾忌医。

【English Translation】

Suspending good doings just because of occasionally suffering unjustified criticism from the surrounding fellows amounts to giving up eating for fear of choking.

Knowing clearly that mistakes should be rectified but contrarily concealing them is the same as refusing to accept treatment for fear that others will know the illness.

139. 幕中之宾　座上之客

139. A trusted person is admitted to participating in decision-making; a distinguished guest is worth inviting to take a prominent seat.

宾入幕中^①，皆沥胆披肝^②之士；客登座上^③，无焦头烂额之人。

【中文注释】　　① 宾入幕中：被允许参与计划制定并提供意见的人。
② 沥胆披肝：肝胆相照；坦诚相见。亦作"披肝沥胆"。
③ 客登座上：座上宾；贵客。

【今文解译】　　凡是能被招入府中密谋要事的幕宾，一定都是可以肝胆相照的人。
凡是能受邀入座上宾席位的客人，一定不是无所作为的泛泛之辈。

【English Translation】

He who is admitted to participating in decision-making must be the one who deserves to be trusted.

He who is invited to take a prominent seat must be the one who is never the cult of the amateur.

140. 种田须尽力　读书要专心

140. Do your best in the field and concentrate your efforts on study.

　　地无余利①，人无余力②，是种田两句要言；心不外驰③，气不外浮④，是读书两句真诀。

【中文注释】　　① 地无余利: 地尽其利, 也即不浪费一寸土地。
　　　　　　　　② 人无余力: 人尽其力; 不遗余力。
　　　　　　　　③ 心不外驰: 心无旁骛。
　　　　　　　　④ 气不外浮: 专心致志。

【今文解译】　　"地无余利" 和 "人无余力" 是种田人的两句要诀。
　　　　　　　　"心不外驰" 和 "气不外浮" 是读书人的两句要诀。

【English Translation】

Turn all the land sources to best account. Let everyone do his best in the field. These are the two maxims for farm work.
Bend the whole mind to the gist. Exert every effort to the key points. These are the two knacks for reading books.

141. 要栽培子弟　勿暴殄天物

141. Bring up your children with care and don't let things go to waste.

　　成就人才，即是栽培子弟；暴殄天物^①，自应折磨儿孙^②。

【中文注释】　① 暴殄天物: 不知爱惜财物，任意浪费东西。
　　　　　　　② 折磨儿孙: 殃及后代。

【今文解译】　成就人才就是将子弟培养成有用的人。
　　　　　　　暴殄天物就是将祸害留给自己的后代。

【English Translation】

To make an accomplished man is to train a disciple of yours to a talent.
To let things go to waste is to bring disaster to the future generations.

142. 和气待人　藏器待时

142. Treat others kindly and don't use your talent till the right time comes.

和气迎人①，平情应物②。抚心希古③，藏器待时④。

【中文注释】　　① 迎人：与人相处。

　　　　　　　　② 平情应物：平情，平心静气；应物，待人接物。

　　　　　　　　③ 抚心希古：抚心，让心保持平静；希古，仰慕古人。

　　　　　　　　④ 藏器待时：器，指才华。意为怀才以待见用。

【今文解译】　　与人相处要和和气气，处理事情要平心静气。

　　　　　　　　学习古人要收敛心性，守住才华以等待时机。

【English Translation】

In getting along with others, be as gentle as possible.
In handling affairs, be calm and collected.
Quiet your heart by following the examples of the ancients.
Don't use your talent till the right time comes.

143. 大好光阴　切莫错过

143. Don't miss the good time when it is with you.

矮板凳，且坐着；好光阴，莫错过。

【中文注释】　本篇意为："条件不具备时，要耐得住寂寞；好光景来临时，不可轻易错过。"

【今文解译】　有个小板凳且先坐下。遇到好光景切莫错过。

【English Translation】

Just take a seat even if only a low stool is available. Do not miss the good time when it is with you.

144. 不失良心　但行正路

144. Keep conscience only to follow the right path.

天地生人，都有一个良心，苟丧此良心，则其去禽兽不远矣。

圣贤教人，总是一条正路，若舍此正路，则常行荆棘之中矣。

【今文解译】　生于天地之间的人类，个个都有一颗良心，如果丧失了这颗良心，那么离禽兽也就不远了。

圣贤教导世人，总是给他们指出一条正路，如果偏离了这条正路，就会常常身陷困厄之中。

【English Translation】

Human beings are born between the heaven and earth, each bearing a good sense. Without the good sense they would not be far from becoming beasts.

The sage instructs the multitude by directing a right way for them. Let them follow the said right way, or they will travel in the land of thistles and thorns.

145. 务本业者常乐　当大任者常忧

145. He who focuses on his own business is always happy; he who is in charge always worried.

世之言乐者，但曰读书乐、田家乐。可知务本业①者，其境常安。

古之言忧者，必曰天下忧、廊庙忧。可知当大任者，其心良苦。

【中文注释】　　① 本业：儒家倡导的本业就是指务农和读书，也即"耕读"。

【今文解译】　　世人只要谈及"快乐"二字，就一定会提到读书之乐和种田之乐。由此可见，专务本业的人，其生活才是充满安乐的。
　　　　　　　　古时候的人只要一谈起"忧患"二字，就必定会提及天下之忧和朝廷之忧；由此可知，担当大事者，其用心实在良苦。

【English Translation】

When talking about pleasures people would normally refer to those of reading books and doing farm work. From this we know that only those who have done well in their lines of business are enabled to enjoy plenty of real pleasures thereby.

When talking about cares the ancients would mostly refer to those for the state affairs and court affairs as well. From this we know that those who are entrusted with important tasks must have really given much thought to their duties.

146. 求死难救　求福在己

146. It's hard to save a person who is determined to end his life; to seek happiness, do it by oneself.

天虽好生[①]，亦难救求死之人；人能造福，即可邀悔祸之天。

【中文注释】　① 好生：乐见万物之生，而不乐见万物之死。

【今文解译】　上天虽然有好生之德，但却无法挽救一个一心求死的人的性命。
人如果能够创造幸福，就连上天也会为它所造成的灾祸而懊恼。

【English Translation】

The heaven takes pleasure in the welfare of living things, but if requested to save a person who is determined to end his life with death, it can do nothing to help.
When humans are capable of creating happiness to the world, even the heaven will be moved to regret for the calamities it has brought about.

147. 身不正难有好子弟　依势者必有真对头

147. Your children will behave well if you yourself stand straight; bully others on another's strength and one will bring in enemies for himself.

薄族者，必无好儿孙；薄师者，必无佳子弟。君所见亦多矣。

恃力者，忽逢真敌手；恃势者，忽逢大对头。人所料不及也。

【今文解译】　苛待族人的人，必无孝悌忠信的子孙后代；不尊敬师长的人，一定教不出优秀的弟子。这样的情形真是见得太多了。

好仗力欺人的人，说不准哪天会碰到强劲的敌手；好仗势欺人的人，说不准哪天会遇到势力更大的对头。世事难料啊！

【 English Translation 】

It always follows that those who treat their relatives harshly can never bring up their own filial offspring, and that those who fail to respect their teachers can never breed good disciples of their own.

It is unexpected but quite natural that one will meet one's match if one has a liking for showing one's strength, and that one will encounter a strong opponent if one has a habit to throw one's weight around.

148. 为学要静敬　教人去骄惰

148. To learn is to make yourself quiet and respectful; to educate people is to get rid of their complacency and laziness.

为学①不外静敬②二字，教人③先去骄惰④二字。

【中文注释】　① 为学：做学问；致力于学习。

② 静敬：沉静的心与敬畏的态度。

③ 教人：教导他人；教书育人。

④ 骄惰：骄傲自满和懒惰倦怠。

【今文解译】　做学问不外乎认准两个字："静"与"敬"。

教书先教学生戒除两个字："骄"与"惰"。

【English Translation】

In academic research, what one should have are no more than a quiet mind and a reverent manner.

To teach students, one should first instruct them to remove complacency and laziness from within.

149. 面对知己无愧　读书要能致用

149. Be worthy of your confidant and practice what you have learned.

人得一知己，须对知己而无惭①；士既多读书，必求读书而有用②。

【中文注释】　① 无惭: 没有愧疚之感。
　　　　　　　② 有用: 付诸实践。

【今文解译】　人若有幸得一知己，就一定要无愧于这位知己。
　　　　　　　志学者既然博览群书，那一定要做到学以致用。

【English Translation】

Having made a confidant, one should be worthy of him.
Having read widely, a scholar must try his best to put what he has learned into practice.

150. 直道教人　诚心待人

150. Educate people to follow the right path and treat them with sincerity.

以直道教人，人即不从，而自反无愧，切勿曲以求容①也；以诚心待人，人或不谅②，而历久自明，不必急于求白③也。

【中文注释】　① 曲以求容：结合前述文字，可理解为"以改变初衷而求得妥协"。
② 不谅：不谅解；不理解。
③ 求白：解释；说明。

【今文解译】　教人要教正面的东西，即使别人听不进去，自我反省时也不至于感到惭愧，切不可改变初衷去迎合别人。
你用诚意待人，别人或许不一定领情，但是时间久了他们会明白你的诚意的，没有必要急着去表白自己。

【English Translation】

Instruct people with righteousness, and you will feel no sorry when reflecting yourself. Never stoop down to make a compromise on your part even if they do not listen to you.

People may not understand at the very beginning the sincerity you treat them with, but may do in the end as time goes by. So, there is no need for you to be rash for explanation.

151. 粗粝能甘　纷华不染

151. Be a man who can live a simple life and resist the temptation of wealth and rank.

粗粝能甘，必是有为之士；纷华不染，方称杰出之人。

【今文解译】　过着简朴的生活，内心却充满快乐，这样的人一定是有作
为的人。
身处荣华富贵之地，思想却不受其熏染，这样的人才是杰
出的人。

【English Translation】

He who lives a simple life and can still take it as pleasure must be the one who
is promising in his career.

He who lives amid fame and wealth and can still withstand the temptations
thereof must be the one who is prominent.

152. 性情执拗 不可谋事

152. One cannot collaborate with those who are of stubborn temperament.

性情执拗之人，不可与谋事也；机趣流通①之士，始可与言文②也。

【中文注释】 ① 机趣流通：机趣，意似趣味、情趣、志趣；流通，意似灵通豁达。合在一起可简约为"志趣通达"。
② 可与言文：可以聚在一起谈论文化或文艺。

【今文解译】 性情固执乖戾的人，不可与其共事。
机趣灵通豁达的人，方可与其言文。

【English Translation】

One cannot collaborate with those who are of stubborn temperament.
One can only discuss literature with those who are of taste and open-mindedness.

153. 做人不必事事皆能

153. There is no need to be capable of doing everything.

不必于世事件件皆能，惟求与古人心心相印。

【今文解译】 不必什么事都能干，但求与古人心心相印。

【 English Translation 】

There is no need to be capable of doing everything, but a need to share the same mind with the ancient sages.

154. 无愧于心　收效桑榆

154. Be worthy of yourself and strive to gain some exploits before getting too old.

夙夜①所为，得毋抱惭于衾影②；光阴已逝，尚期收效③于桑榆④。

【中文注释】　① 夙夜：早晚；从早到晚。
② 衾影：《宋史》蔡元定传："独行不愧影，独寝不愧衾。"
③ 收效：收获；有所作为。
④ 桑榆：比喻晚年；垂老之年。

【今文解译】　一天的所作所为，夜晚睡觉时要不感到惭愧才好。
尽管韶华已逝，但还是有人在晚年想着有所作为。

【English Translation】

When sleeping alone in the dead of night, one should feel no qualms about what he has done by daytime.
The better part of life has passed, but some people are still longing for further exploits in their later years.

155. 创业维艰　毋负先人

155. It's hard to start a business, so we should not let our ancestors down.

　　念祖考创家基，不知栉风沐雨①，受多少苦辛，才能足食足衣，以贻后世。

　　为子孙计长久，除却读书耕田，恐别无生活，总期克勤克俭，毋负先人。

【中文注释】　　① 栉风沐雨：形容工作辛苦，借风梳发，借雨洗头。

【今文解译】　　祖先为创立家族的基业，不知栉风沐雨吃了多少苦，才让家人过上丰衣足食的生活，还有家财留与后世。
　　　　　　　　子孙后代的长久之计，除了读书种地恐没有其他的谋生手段，总希望他们能克勤克俭，不要辜负了祖先。

【 English Translation 】

The well-being of family property, with which the sons and grandsons are enabled to live a life of ample food and clothing, is what their forefathers brought about by going through all the untold hardships.

Study for official career or work in the field is probably the only choice to make a life for long. So, the descendants are always instructed to practice thrift in order to live worthy of their forefathers' hardworking.

156. 生要有济于乡里　死要有可传之事

156. Try to be helpful to your native fellows when alive and do something worth remembering after death.

　　但作里中不可少之人，便为于世有济；必使身后有可传之事，方为此生不虚。

【今文解译】　　能成为乡里乡亲不可或缺的人，就是有益于社会的人。
　　　　　　　　有了值得别人缅怀称颂的事迹，人这辈子才算没白活。

【English Translation】

The man indispensable to his native place must be the one who has made contributions to the society.

The man who is worthy to be remembered after death must be the one who did not spend his life in vain.

157. 齐家先修身　读书在明理

157. The government of a man's family should be preceded by his self-cultivation; to acquire knowledge is to refine sensibility.

齐家先修身，言行不可不慎；读书在明理，识见不可不高。

【今文解译】　齐家必先修身，一言一行不可不慎。
　　　　　　　读书在于明理，所识所见不可不高。

【 English Translation 】

The government of a man's family should be preceded by his self-cultivation.
To do it well he must never be too cautious about his words and deeds.
The purpose of reading books is to refine a man's sensibility. When he ponders issues his knowledge and experience should be better than average.

158. 积善有余庆　多藏必厚亡

158. Things good for the world enjoy constant prosperity while too much amassment is liable to lead to great loss.

桃实之肉暴于外，不自吝惜，人得取而食之；食之而种其核，犹饶生气①焉，此可见积善者有余庆②也。

栗实之肉秘于内，深自防护，人乃剖而食之；食之而弃其壳，绝无生理矣，此可知多藏者必厚亡也。

【中文注释】　① 犹饶生气：生机勃勃。

② 积善者有余庆：语自"积善之家，必有余庆；积不善之家，必有余殃"。意即修善积德的个人和家庭，必然有更多的吉庆；作恶坏德的，必有更多的祸殃。

【今文解译】　桃子的果肉袒露在外面，毫不吝啬，人人皆可取而食之。食后还能把它的核种在泥土里，以孕育新的生命。由此可见，做善事者，其吉庆一定源远流长。

栗子的果肉深藏于壳内，自我保护极好，人们只有将其破开才能食用。食后将它的壳扔了，壳成了没用的东西。由此可见，藏得越多的，损失也就越大。

【English Translation】

With its pulp generously exposed to light, the peach is to be bitten directly when people get it. After the pulp is eaten up, the seed will be replanted in the soil, and will then grow vigorously with the passage of time. From this we see that things good for the world enjoy constant prosperity.

With the pulp closely stored within the shell, the chestnut needs to be cut from without when people want to eat it. After the kernel is eaten up, the shell will be thrown away, and will hopelessly stay where it is and die out once for all. From this we know that too much amassment is liable to lead to great loss.

159. 修身求备　读书求深

159. Perfection to a man's self-cultivation is applicable and so profoundness to his academic pursuit.

　　求备①之心，可用之以修身，不可用之以接物；知足之心，可用之以处境，不可用之以读书。

【中文注释】　　① 求备：追求完美。

【今文解译】　　追求完美的想法可以用在修身养性上，但不可用在待人接物上。
　　　　　　　　知足的心理可以用在日常生活上，但不可用在读书学习上。

【English Translation】

Seeking perfection is applicable to a man's self-cultivation but not applicable to his social dealings.

A contented mind is applicable to a man's daily life but not applicable to his academic research.

160. 立言与立功立德并传

160. Establishing arguments is as important as cultivating virtue and making achievements.

有守虽无所展布^①，而其节不挠，故与有猷有为而并重^②；立言^③即未经起行，而于人有益，故与立功立德而并传^④。

【中文注释】　①展布：陈述；展现。
②并重：同样重要。
③立言：此处喻所倡导的学说、观点、观念或思想等。
④并传：一起被传颂。

【今文解译】　拥有良好的操守虽然不足为道，然而那种坚持操守的百折不挠的精神，却堪与有谋有为并重。
所著述的学说即使尚未得到实践验证，但只要对人民大众是有益的，也堪与立功立德并传。

【English Translation】

A man's sticking to moral principles may not be worth saying, but if he can do so under any circumstances, even without making any contributions, he is still spiritually eligible to share the same honor with those who have done something to contribute.

Those who expound their ideas in writing and make people benefit from them, even not yet put into practice, still deserve to be praised together with the ones who have succeeded in extending their virtue and rendering a meritorious service.

161. 求教受劝　向善积德

161. To consult is to ask for advice; to do good is to accumulate virtue.

遇老成人①，便肯殷殷求教②，则向善必笃③也；听切实话④，觉得津津有味，则进德⑤可期也。

【中文注释】　① 老成人：有阅历、有德行的老者。
② 殷殷：诚恳；热切。
③ 笃：坚定不移。
④ 切实话：实实在在的话。
⑤ 进德：德业方面的进步。

【今文解译】　遇到年高德劭的人就走上前去虚心讨教，向善之心可谓至笃至诚。
听到实实在在的话心里便觉得津津有味，修身进德可期有所造诣。

【English Translation】

That one would modestly ask for advice from the aged of rich experience and moral integrity at every turn is the manifestation of earnestness in his heart for good.

He who would give heed to the honest words with great interest must be the one who can be expected to make progress at any time in his self-cultivation.

162.　有真涵养　写大文章

162. Writing an article of great significance and influence needs genuine accomplishment.

　　有真性情^①，须有真涵养^②；有大识见^③，乃有大文章^④。

【中文注释】　① 真性情: 至真无妄的心性与情思。
　　　　　　　② 真涵养: 真正的修养水平; 真正的涵养功夫。
　　　　　　　③ 大识见: 远大的见识; 高瞻远瞩。
　　　　　　　④ 大文章: 意义非凡、影响广大的文章。

【今文解译】　人要有诚实无欺的真性情, 必须先有积深如渊的真涵养。
　　　　　　　具备了高瞻远瞩的大识见, 才能写出惊世骇俗的大文章。

【English Translation】

To have genuine accomplishment one must first ensure one's cultivation in real earnest.
To write an article of great significance and influence one should first have a great insight.

163. 为善在让　立身在敬

163. To do good is to make a concession; to stand upright is to act with reverence.

　　为善之端^①无尽，只讲一让^②字，便人人可行；立身之道何穷，只得一敬^③字，便事事皆整^④。

【中文注释】　① 端：方式。
　　　　　　　② 让：忍让；退让；谦让；礼让。
　　　　　　　③ 敬：敬畏。
　　　　　　　④ 整：顺当。

【今文解译】　好事是做不完的，只要懂得了"让"字的道理，那么人人都可以做好事。
　　　　　　　立身处世的方法有许多，只要把"敬"字放在心里，做事就没有不顺的。

【English Translation】

There is no ending in doing good things. Knowing how to make a concession everyone can do what he thinks good.

The ways of a man's personal establishment are many. To act with reverence the things he is engaged in will run smooth.

164. 是非自明　得失自知

164. One should have a clear sense of right and wrong and the knowledge about his own merit and demerit.

　　自己所行之是非，尚不能知，安望^①知人？古人已往之得失^②，且不必论，但须论己。

【中文注释】　　① 安望：安，怎么、怎能；望，指望。
② 得失：本意为"得与失"，但此处将其解读为"功过"应该更加贴切。

【今文解译】　　一个连自己的所作所为都不知对错的人，又怎能指望他去理解别人的行为呢?！
古人既往的功过暂且可以不论，但是必须要对自己的功过有一个清醒的认识。

【English Translation】

How can a man be expected to know others clearly and correctly if he cannot tell right or wrong of his own deeds?
There is no need for us to comment on the merits and demerits of the ancients, but a need to assess those of our own.

165. 仁义宽厚　儒家之道

165. Benevolence and tolerance are part of the core of Confucianism.

治术必本儒术者，念念皆仁厚也；今人不及古人者，事事皆虚浮也。

【今文解译】　治理的方略一定要遵从儒学，因为儒家所倡导的都是仁
爱与宽厚。
现代人之所以不如古代人，那是因为现代人所作所为都
华而不实。

【English Translation】

To work out the policies suitable for administration one must resort to
Confucianism, for what Confucianism advocates are all related to benevolence
and tolerance.

The reason why the moderns are inferior to the ancients is just because of the
fact that the moderns are always doing things in a superficial and exaggerating
way.

166. 莫大之祸 起于不忍

166. Almost every big disaster is caused by a momentary lack of tolerance.

莫大之祸，起于须臾之不忍，不可不谨。

【今文解译】　再大的灾祸，都是因为当事人一时不能忍耐而造成的，切不可掉以轻心。

【English Translation】

No matter how sreat the disaster is, it is caused by a momentary lack of tolerance. One can never be too careful to guard against it.

167. 体察他人　换位思考

167. To understand others, one must observe them in their positions.

家之长幼，皆倚赖于我，我亦尝体其情否也？士之衣食，皆取资于人，人亦曾受其益否也？

【今文解译】　家中老小的生活都依靠我，我又何曾体察过他们的情感诉求呢？

读书人的衣食都有赖于别人的劳动，别人是否也曾获益于他呢？

【English Translation】

All the family members, old and young, are dependent on me for daily expenses. Have I ever duly observed their true feelings or appeals?

The food and clothing of a scholar are all in debt to the laboring of others. Is there any of them who has been favored by him?

168. 读书积德　事长亲贤

168. Accumulate virtue while learning; serve the old while paying homage to the worthy.

　　富不肯读书，贵不肯积德，错过可惜也！少不肯事长，愚不肯亲贤，不祥莫大焉！

【今文解译】　生活富裕了却不肯读书，地位高贵了却不肯积德，如此有可为而不为的现象实在令人痛心疾首！
年少时不肯伺奉长辈，智穷时不肯请教贤者，这种不肯事长、不愿亲贤的行为实在不是好兆头！

【English Translation】

What a pity it is that one is unwilling to spend time on study when rich or unwilling to do good turns and dispense charities when in power!
How unfortunate it is that one is reluctant to take care of the aged when young or reluctant to go to the wise for counsel when at one's wit's end!

169. 虞舜立五伦　朱熹集四书

169. The Five Interpersonal Relationships were set by King Shun and the Four Books systematized by Zhu Xi.

　　自虞廷①立五伦②为教③，然后天下有大经；自紫阳④集四子成书⑤，然后天下有正学。

【中文注释】　①虞廷：虞舜，中国上古时代的部落联盟首领，被后世尊为帝，列入"五帝"。
　　②五伦：即父子有亲，君臣有义，夫妇有别，长幼有序，朋友有信。
　　③为教：用以教导和育化民众。
　　④紫阳：北宋理学大家朱熹，字元晦，孔孟学说集大成者。学者称其为紫阳先生。
　　⑤四子成书：朱熹所集注的《论语》《孟子》《大学》和《中庸》，合称"四书"。

【今文解译】　虞舜创立五伦为教，从此天下也就有了历万世而不可易的人伦大法。
　　朱熹集四子之大成，从此世间也就有了可奉为百代圭臬的中正国学。

【English Translation】

King Shun* established the Five Interpersonal Relationships* to fix the precedence between people, and from then on there have existed in the world the ethical principles of human relations.

Zhu Xi* succeeded in systematizing Confucianism with the Four Books*, and since then there have come into being the authoritative criteria followed by all branches of knowledge.

【English Annotation】

* King Shun (c. 2277BC-c. 2178BC), named Yao Chonghua, a legendary sage

king in China's remote antiquity and one of the Five August Emperors in the time before the existence of the Xia Dynasty (c. 3000BC-c. 2100BC), also known as Di Shun or Emperor Shun.

* The Five Interpersonal Relations are referred to those between monarch and subject, father and son, husband and wife, between brothers and between friends.

* Zhu Xi (1130-1200), styled Yuanhui or Zhonghui, a neo-Confucian, thinker, philosopher and educationist of the Southern Song Dynasty, also known as Zhu Zi and famed as the master of Confucianism known next to Confucius and Mencius.

* The Four Books are referred to the Chinese classic texts illustrating the core value and belief systems in Confucianism, including *Analects of Confucius, Mencius, Great Learning* and *The Mean*, which were made the core of the official curriculum for the civil service examinations.

170. 意趣清高　志量远大

170. Be a man of noble interest and great aspiration.

意趣①清高，利禄不能动②也；志量③远大，富贵不能淫④也。

【中文注释】　① 意趣：意兴和情趣。
② 动：使动摇；撼动。
③ 志量：心志和度量。
④ 淫：放纵；毫无约束。

【今文解译】　意趣清淡高雅，即使面对钱财和爵禄也不为所动。
志量阔远宏大，纵然身在富贵中也丝毫不改本色。

【English Translation】

So long as a man keeps aloof from petty politics and material pursuits, neither rank nor wealth can change his mind.

So long as a man has high aspirations and far-sight, neither riches nor honor can lead him to immoderate activities.

171. 势家女难伺　富家儿难处

171. It's hard to serve a daughter from a powerful family and get along with a son of a rich clan.

最不幸者，为势家女作翁姑；最难处者，为富家儿作师友。

【今文解译】　最不幸的是给有权有势人家的女儿当公婆。
　　　　　　　最难的是给有钱人家的子弟做老师或朋友。

【English Translation】

It's the most unfortunate thing to be the parents-in-law of the daughter of a powerful family.
It's the most difficult thing to be the tutor or friend of the son of a rich family.

172. 钱造福也能生祸　药救人也能杀人

172. Money can do man good and harm as well; drugs can save people and kill as well.

　　钱能福人，亦能祸人，有钱者不可不知；药能生人，亦能杀人，用药者不可不慎。

【今文解译】　　钱能给人带来福祉，也能给人带来祸害，有钱的人对此不可不知。
药能用来救人性命，也能用来取人性命，用药的人切不可不谨慎。

【English Translation】

Money can do man good and harm as well. So, those who are rich in money should be aware of the untowardness clearly.
Drugs can save people and kill as well. So, those who prescribe drugs should know the duality and be careful anyhow.

173. 身体力行　集思广益

173. To solve a problem collectively, one should do it without letup and listen to all the useful opinions.

　　凡事勿徒委于人，必身体力行，方能有济；凡事不可执于己，必集思广益，乃罔后艰。

【今文解译】　不要什么事都交人去办，一定要身体力行，这样才能成为一个有用的人。

不要做什么事都固执己见，一定要集思广益，这样才会不惧怕任何困难。

【English Translation】

Do not assign everything to others. Only by doing things yourself can you become a person useful to the public.

Do not adhere stubbornly to your own views in doing things. Draw on collective wisdom and absorb all useful ideas, and you will be afraid of no difficulties.

174. 种田读书　皆成其业

174. Farm work and study for officialdom are the two ways to earn a living.

　　耕读固是良谋，必工课无荒，乃能成其业；仕宦虽称贵显，若官箴有玷，亦未见其荣。

【今文解译】　种地读书固然是理想的谋生之道，但一定要种地读书两不误，才能成就未来的事业。

入仕为官固然可以光耀门楣，但若辱没了自己的官声，为官的荣耀也就荡然无存了。

【English Translation】

Farm work and study for officialdom are the two good ways to earn a living, but they can only be so when both are fulfilled absolutely.

To be a scholarly official is known as glorification, but if one brings disgrace to the title conferred, the said glorification will crumble to dust.

175. 儒者多文为富　君子疾名不称

175. A Confucian scholar takes the productiveness of his writings as wealth; an accomplished man is always afraid that he cannot live up to his reputation.

儒者多文为富，其文非时文也；君子疾名不称，其名非科名也。

【今文解译】　儒家学者将多写文章看作是自己积累的财富，而这里所说的文章并不是指应景之作。

正人君子生怕自己盛名之下其实难副，而这里所说的名声并不是指科举榜上的排名。

【English Translation】

A Confucian scholar takes the productiveness of his writings as wealth, but none of which refers to the words of the occasion.

An accomplished man is afraid of not matching the fame he has earned, which by no means the ranking in imperial examinations.

176. 博学笃志　神闲气静

176. Learn widely and aspire steadfastly; be calm-minded and mild-mannered.

　　博学笃志^①，切问近思^②，此八字是收放心的功夫；神闲气静^③，智深勇沉^④，此八字是干大事的本领。

【中文注释】　　① 博学笃志：博学多闻，志向坚定。
　　　　　　　　② 切问近思：请教恳切，思考缜密。
　　　　　　　　③ 神闲气静：心神闲逸，气息安静。
　　　　　　　　④ 智深勇沉：智谋深远，勇敢沉着。

【今文解译】　　"博学笃志"和"切问近思"，这八个字是一个人做学问必下的功夫。
　　　　　　　　"神闲气静"和"智深勇沉"，这八个字是一个人干大事必备的素质。

【English Translation】

Learn widely, aspire steadfastly, inquire earnestly, and think carefully, — these are the four mental qualities indispensable in academic researching.
Be leisurely-minded, be mild-mannered, be deep-witted, and be cool-headed, — these are the four inner powers badly needed in handling major issues.

177. 规我过者益友　偏私我者小人

177. He who admonishes me of my errors is a helpful friend and a mean fellow, he who only pursues his own ends.

　　何者为益友？凡事肯规我之过者是也。何者为小人？凡事必徇己之私者是也。

【今文解译】　什么样的人称得上是益友？肯规劝我改正过错的人就是益友。

什么样的人是小人？什么事都为自己私利考虑的人就是小人。

【English Translation】

What kind of person is a helpful friend? He who is ready to admonish me of my errors is a helpful friend.

What kind of person is a mean fellow? He who pursues his own ends at every turn is a mean fellow.

178. 待人宜宽　行礼宜厚

178. Be lenient when treating with others and generous when sending gifts.

待人宜宽，惟待子孙不可宽；行礼宜厚，惟行嫁娶不必厚。

【今文解译】　对待别人要宽容，但是对待自己的子孙不能宽容。
礼尚往来要厚重，但是迎娶送嫁则不必太过铺张。

【English Translation】

One should be lenient with others but should not be lenient with the sons and grandsons of one's own.
Courtesy should be fully observed, while wedding should not be arranged too extravagantly and wastefully.

179. 观已然而知未然

179. Look at what has happened, and you will know what will happen.

事但观其已然，便可知其未然；人必尽其当然，乃可听其自然。

【今文解译】　观察已经发生的事物，就可知道接下来将会发生什么。
一个人只有先尽其本分，才能听任其按自然规律发展。

【English Translation】

Look at what has happened, and you will know what will happen.
Only by doing his part first can a man be let have his own way.

180. 观规模之大小　知事业之高卑

180. Look at its size effect, and you will know if an enterprise is
flourishing or declining.

　　观规模之大小，可以知事业之高卑；察德泽之深浅，可以知门祚之
久暂。

【今文解译】　　看一下规模气势，就知道一家企业是兴旺发达还是停滞
　　　　　　　　萎缩。
　　　　　　　　观察一下德泽深浅，就知道一户人家的家运是绵长还是
　　　　　　　　短暂。

【English Translation】

Look at its size effect, and you will know if an enterprise is flourishing or
declining.
Observe the level of a family's charity, and you will know if its fortune can
last or not.

181. 君子尚义　小人趋利

181. A gentleman upholds morality and justice while a mean fellow pursues interests.

　　义之中有利，而尚义之君子，初非计及于利也；利之中有害，而趋利之小人，并不愿其为害也。

【今文解译】　道义之中也有利益，而崇尚道义的君子，最初并非冲着利益而去。
利益之中也有弊处，而唯利是图的小人，并不希望弊处殃及自己。

【English Translation】

There are advantages in moral cultivation. But the gentleman, when cultivating morality, doesn't have the intention to go for the advantages therein.
There are disadvantages in pursuit of interests. But the base man, when pursuing interests, doesn't expect that it will bring disadvantages to him.

182. 小心谨慎无咎　高位难保其终

182. Be careful to avoid error, for superiority gained through a high position cannot last long.

小心谨慎者，必善其后，畅则无咎也；高自位置得，难保其终，亢则有悔也。

【今文解译】　小心谨慎的人，做事一定会有始有终，只要按事物的发展规律行事，就绝不会犯错。

优越是因为位高权重，终究难保长久，如果因此而变得骄横起来，总有一天会后悔。

【English Translation】

He who is prudent in action must know well how to see a thing through: Act in accordance with natural laws and one will make no error.

Superiority gained through a high position cannot last long: He who thinks himself great because of his high position will repent someday.

183. 勿以耕读谋富贵

183. One should not take farm work and academic research as the means to accumulate riches and glory.

耕所以养生，读所以明道，此耕读之本原也，而后世乃假以谋富贵矣。

衣取其蔽体，食取其充饥，此衣食之实用也，而时人乃藉以逞豪奢矣。

【今文解译】 种田是为了维持生计，读书是为了明白事理，这是种田读书的根本目的，可是后世的人们却借此谋取富贵。
穿衣是为了蔽体御寒，吃饭是为了充饥果腹，这是穿衣吃饭的实用性，可是现在的人却在衣食上极尽奢华。

【English Translation】

To do farm work is to earn a livelihood. To read books is to attain the knowledge of the world. These are the purposes the two ancient trades are done for; nevertheless, the young generations use them as the means to accumulate riches and glory.

Clothing is made to shelter physical bodies. Food is prepared to stave off hunger. These are the practical functions clothing and food are worked on, but people of the time do everything possible thereby to show off extravagance and luxury.

184. 富而不懂布置则耻

184. It's a shame if one wishes to make plenty of money but know not how to use it.

人皆欲贵也，请问一官到手，怎样施行？人皆欲富也，且问万贯缠腰，如何布置？

【今文解译】　人人都想有显赫的地位，但是请问：就是给你个官当，你又将如何行使手中的权力呢？

人人都想变得富有，但是请问：即使让你拥有万贯家产，你又将如何使用你的财富呢？

【English Translation】

Everyone desires to have a high rank. But the question is: what do you do if you are really high-ranked?

Everyone wishes to be rich. But the question is: how do you use your money if you are extremely rich?